Praise for *A Teachable Spirit*

A Teachable Spirit is a profound and timely invitation to rediscover humility in a world saturated with arrogance and noise. A.J. Swoboda's insights are both challenging and liberating, reminding us that authentic discipleship begins with a heart willing to learn from anyone, anywhere. I was personally irritated, convicted, poked, prodded, and pressed into greater curiosity—a sure sign of a deep and rich book. I know it'll be helpful to you too.

> Chuck DeGroat, PhD, professor of pastoral care and
> Christian spirituality, licensed professional counselor,
> and author of *When Narcissism Comes to Church*

We live in a world of broken specializations. Social media curates our audience until it becomes people who say only what gets our attention; scientism listens only to scientists; sociologists want to know which studies prove which politicians or issues women voted for; theologians require others to express themselves in theological terms and do so with accuracy. Specialists look for other specialists. Don't we all encounter a critic on some social media and look to see who wrote it? *Do they have the credentials to say that about me?* A.J. Swoboda prophetically cuts into these broken specializations and heals the flow of learning to the capacity and humility to listen to everyone.

> Scot McKnight, professor of New Testament
> and author of *A Church Called Tov*

In a world increasingly defined by echo chambers, A.J. Swoboda offers a timely and compelling call to cultivate a teachable spirit. Through captivating stories and profound wisdom, he inspires us to embrace humility and curiosity and to learn from everyone—friends, strangers, children, and even our enemies. This transformative book is essential for anyone seeking to follow Jesus faithfully in a polarized age.

> Ken Shigematsu, pastor of Tenth Church, Vancouver,
> BC, and author of *God in My Everything*

In a "you do you" world paralyzed by relativism on the one hand and seduced by certainty on the other, the virtue of teachability is rare. Are we willing to admit that we have much to learn? A.J. Swoboda urges us to be willing to learn from experts, strangers, children, parents, the dead, enemies, and the wider culture. Our collective future depends on it.

Carmen Joy Imes, associate professor of Old Testament, Talbot School of Theology, Biola University

In an age of content, we are quickly losing one of the great gifts of human experience—*curiosity*. To live well, we must learn well. Better yet, we must acquire and embrace the *desire* to learn—a living, breathing curiosity about God, ourselves, and our world. A.J. Swoboda offers a compelling call and an accessible path to living the life of a learner, not simply to *know more*, but to *become more*. As Swoboda concludes, "The goal, then, for disciples of Jesus is not to get more information from the teacher. The goal is to become like him." This book shows us how.

Jay Y. Kim, pastor and author of *Analog Church* and *Listen, Listen, Speak*

In a world rife with entrenched beliefs and divisive echo chambers, A.J. Swoboda offers a profound perspective on the art of learning and what it means to be apprentices of Jesus, to be his "TAs." With captivating prose and poignant personal stories, he demonstrates how authentic Christian discipleship demands a radical humility—the willingness to learn from anyone, anywhere, anytime. From scholars and strangers to adversaries and ancient wisdom, Swoboda invites us to embrace the kind of intellectual curiosity that characterizes true followers of Jesus. This isn't just another book about learning; it's a call to cultivate the most vital (and often overlooked) virtue of our time—a truly teachable spirit. It's not just a book you'll read; it's one you'll live.

Leonard Sweet, author, professor, preacher, publisher, proprietor, and founder of SpiritVenture Ministries

When teachability and humility have gone out of fashion as a virtue for Christians or as a sign of serious scholarship, this is the book we need to call us back to who we are. Christians are called to be learners, not only first, but always. A teachable spirit is a spirit of a Christ follower. A.J. Swoboda invites us to return to the humility of being a learner not only of our heroes but also of our enemies in order to know how to think, and how to think well. In this transformative book, we are challenged to the posture of a true disciple—a learner.

Rev. Dr. Sarah Baldwin, vice president of Student Life, Asbury University, and author of *Generation Awakened*

Christians by definition are learners. We follow Jesus, our Teacher. How can we love God with our heart and soul and mind if we are unwilling to learn? In *A Teachable Spirit*, A.J. Swoboda is our guide to guides. He encourages us to be lifelong learners and shows us that we have something we can learn from everyone.

Ian Harber, author of *Walking Through Deconstruction*, writer, and Christian media producer

Once again, A.J. Swoboda has given us a great gift toward becoming mature disciples of Jesus Christ. Being teachable is at the heart of discipleship, but it's often only an abstraction. Swoboda gives wise direction so we can learn from a wide range of people. I particularly appreciated his chapter on learning from enemies, a most challenging assignment. Do yourself a favor and invest in developing a teachable spirit.

Gerry Breshears, PhD, professor of theology, Western Seminary, Portland, Oregon

In *A Teachable Spirit*, A.J. Swoboda humbly demonstrates that "to be teachable is to allow someone else to love you." Having known him for a few years, I can say that his life embodies this message too. Though he is exponentially smarter than me, he consistently asks me more questions (seemingly genuinely curiously!) than I think to ask him. From his written and lived example, I've learned how to learn even from my ideological and theological "enemies" in a manner that exudes both love of and loving allegiance to the person of Christ. The body of Christ needs this book.

Evan Wickham, lead pastor, Park Hill Church

a Teachable Spirit

The Virtue of Learning from Strangers,
Enemies, and Absolutely Anyone

A.J. Swoboda

ZONDERVAN
REFLECTIVE

The illiterate of the twenty-first century
will not be those who cannot read and write,
but those who cannot learn, unlearn, and relearn.

Alvin Toffler, *Future Shock*

Contents

Introduction. 1

One   Learning How to Learn. 9

Two   Learning from Experts. 31

Three Learning from Strangers 54

Four   Learning from the Dead 76

Five   Learning from Children. 98

Six   Learning from Parents. 122

Seven Learning from Secular Culture 143

Eight   Learning from Enemies. 164

Conclusion. 185

Acknowledgments 189

Notes 191

Introduction

Spanish has always been my Achilles' heel.

For five years—spanning three years of high school and two at university—I furiously attempted to learn the mother tongue of many of my hometown friends in Keizer, Oregon. Despite studying Spanish for half a decade, the language has all but abandoned me in adulthood, minus a phrase or two that can be used in a pinch. I've lost most of it. Not all languages are this challenging for me. Biblical Greek, given my day job, is a far more familiar and comfortable language. But that pesky Spanish—five years of study, and all I can do is ask if the joint has a bathroom.

I've often wondered, *Will I finally learn Spanish in heaven?*

As silly as it seems, this question is not insignificant. Over a lifetime, every human will accumulate a set of skills that will shape their existence—driving a stick shift, carrying on conversations, doing the finances, putting the green, passing a basketball between the legs, walking and chewing gum at the same time. The list goes on. Be it for survival or a favorite pastime, life offers chance after chance to develop the skills necessary to thrive. So it's not a silly question: Will humans, upon entering the presence of God's glory in heaven, continue to cultivate such skills? Will we learn new things in heaven? And maybe unlearn what we've

1

done wrong our whole life? In short, will I finally be able to learn Spanish in heaven?

The Bible is quiet on this subject. But not silent. In the divinely inspired words of Revelation that paint the picture of a future new creation—that place Christians call "heaven"—John describes what his eyes passingly behold. The apostle catches sight of throngs of worshipers who are, as he describes them, "a great multitude that no one could count, from every nation, tribe, people and language, standing before the throne and before the Lamb" (Revelation 7:9).

John notices that the inhabitants of heaven speak different languages. This is noteworthy, if for no other reason than the divine realm John beholds depicts a human community in all its diversity—ethnic, tribal, and even cultural. For John, heaven does not annihilate linguistic diversity. Which could be bad news. If the possibility of learning new languages isn't a reality in heaven, then we're all relegated to an everlasting existence with others with whom we'll never be able to communicate. That doesn't sound like heaven; it sounds like hell.

The other option is that God will give infinite knowledge to humans in heaven. But wouldn't that entail humans becoming something more than human? Only God can have divine, perfect, infinite knowledge. The triune God is the only know-it-all. So just as resurrection doesn't annihilate difference, neither will it fix our finitude. In heaven, human beings continue to be just that—*beings*.

John's vision isn't the only text we can approach to answer our question about learning in heaven. There's Paul's letter to the Ephesians. At the heart of the epistle, the apostle describes the resurrection state of the follower of Jesus: "God raised us up with Christ and seated us with him in the heavenly realms in

Christ Jesus, in order that in the coming ages he might show the incomparable riches of his grace, expressed in his kindness to us in Christ Jesus" (Ephesians 2:6–7).

Keep in mind that Paul is describing the state of the saint in glory. Notice that God will "show" the resurrected inhabitant's various realities—namely, about the endless bounties of God's grace, kindness, and mercy that went unappreciated on earth. For Paul, God has more to show, reveal, and make manifest to our finite eyes. We will, it seems, *always* have more to learn. Perhaps forever. Heaven, then, is the ongoing education of beholding God's never-ending revelation. Paul's description of the future of a Christian is one in which they have much more to learn—and the Lamb will be their teacher. For those who love to learn, the Christian way should be the best.

There are obstacles to overcome. We may be able to look forward to learning from God forever. In the present, however, we tend to be stubbornly prideful, inflexible, and unteachable. Too often, Christians can fall into a crippling belief that the highest form of learning is in the realms of spiritual and religious knowledge (such as theology, biblical studies, and Christian living). No doubt, these are core components of God's curriculum for our lives. But such a narrow outlook fails to recognize that *everything* in one's life makes up the curriculum of discipleship, from changing the car's oil, loving one's spouse, forgiving a boss, and raising a child to building a treehouse, becoming humble, and even running a business. Following Christ is submitting to the "yoke" of Jesus (Matthew 11:29), not only in the sacred, but equally in the mundane. In other words, a life under the tutelage of the Holy Spirit treats nothing as extracurricular. If life is the curriculum, nothing remains secular.

Christian maturity, in part, comes alongside accepting the

frustrating fact that none of us have arrived at a full understanding of truth. Paul further writes, "Now we see only a reflection as in a mirror; then we shall see face to face. Now I know in part; then I shall know fully, even as I am fully known" (1 Corinthians 13:12). Paul's critical teaching here undermines any possibility for religious arrogance or theological pride. Following Jesus entails a recognition that we do not see clearly. This can too often be forgotten. When arrogance colors Christians' discipleship, it paves the way for miles and miles of pain and frustration for everyone around them.

As a professor, I'm all too familiar with the angst students face when they discover that some of their ideas or beliefs don't hold up to Scripture, reality, or truth. The experience can be dizzying. Studying at the university, one of my students soon discovered through reading, coursework, and conversation that some of the finer points of theology he had been handed by his family of origin simply did not align with what is revealed about God throughout Scripture. As he began to rethink his theology, he shared with his parents his discoveries. Their response was cold, dismissive, and combative. Not only did they interpret their son's learning journey as a threat, but they also came to see it as a rejection of the very faith they had instilled in him. Due to an underlying insecurity, they dismissed his learning as apostasy.

How could this be? A disciple is a learner of the way of Jesus. Sadly, for too many, learning is caricatured as a rejection of the faith when it should be appreciated as a pathway toward a deeper faith. What we so often assume is a "crisis of faith" is really a "crisis of understanding."[1] Loving God is not the end of learning. True learning is loving God with one's mind.

Reality, Dallas Willard once wrote, is "what we humans run into when we are wrong."[2] Reality can be painful. Nobody would disagree that it is difficult to discover that one's present thinking and the truth do not correlate. Still, isn't this a sign that someone is on the right path? Because the Christian is called to relentlessly demolish any high place of theological idolatry—those altars in our minds where we've come to love our thinking about God more than God himself. This demolition project is hard. But it is necessary and liberating. Loving God is not the same as fully understanding him. "Truth is eternal," writes Madeleine L'Engle, "[but] knowledge is changeable. It is disastrous to confuse them."[3] It takes faith to believe in absolute truth. But it takes humility to admit we don't comprehend it absolutely.

Learning includes unlearning. When God calls Jeremiah to his ministry, the prophet is befuddled. How could God call someone so young to be a prophet? "Alas, Sovereign LORD," Jeremiah responds. "I do not know how to speak; I am too young." Then God responds, "Do not say, 'I am too young.' You must go to to everyone I send you to and say whatever I command you" (Jeremiah 1:6–7).

Commentators point out that God never says Jeremiah is wrong. Indeed, by worldly standards, the prophet was young, likely thirteen or fourteen. God doesn't correct Jeremiah's self-knowledge. Rather, God corrects the fact that Jeremiah bases his identity on it. As Old Testament scholar Christopher J. H. Wright reflects, Jeremiah's comments were "true but irrelevant."[4] Jeremiah had to unlearn his entrenched belief that God couldn't use a young person like himself for prophetic work. Jeremiah would be teachable. As a result, his story is recorded for perpetuity. Our problem isn't that we're ignorant or uninformed. Sometimes our knowledge gets in the way of our Christlikeness. Too often, our greater sin is that we're unteachable.

This book is about one of the most challenging characteristics to embody—teachability. It is also about why that virtue is so difficult to cultivate in our fallen state. The "pride of life"—as the apostle John calls it in 1 John 2:16—is the lingering consequence of the cosmic fall on one's intellect. Sin always cripples good thinking. Life without God, Paul writes, is an experience marked by the "futility of their thinking" and being "darkened in their understanding"[5] (Ephesians 4:17–18). Sin, then, is a "veil" that keeps us from seeing as we were meant to.[6] And this veil can only be taken away by Christ. When Paul later wrote that in Christ "are hidden all the treasures of wisdom and knowledge," the statement flowed naturally from his thinking that the way toward a healed mind is through encountering Christ (Colossians 2:3). True and restored thought is possible only by turning toward God. As the pagan king Nebuchadnezzar declared in Daniel, "I, Nebuchadnezzar, raised my eyes toward heaven, and my sanity was restored" (Daniel 4:34). Our minds are fractured by sin. Turning to God begins the restoration.

Christian discipleship should propel us to use our minds more, not less. Thankfully, we have countless luminaries to aid in teaching us how to do so—the most impactful of whom have been shown to be teachable.[7] It's always refreshing to see a renowned theologian passingly comment about their own folly and ignorance.[8] Or to see a hero like Charles Spurgeon confess that the deep thought of a simple cook named Mary King left him transformed:

> I learnt more from her than I should have learned from any six doctors of divinity of the sort we have nowadays. There are some Christian people who taste, and see, and enjoy religion in their souls, and who get at a deeper knowledge of it than books can ever give them, though they should search all their days.[9]

Stories like these embolden our spirits and humble our minds, reminding us that the path toward holy learning will go through whomever God determines. We can, and should, resolve ourselves to learning from whomever God places before us.

What follows are experiments in learning. I will consider seven groups or entities Christians have often struggled to learn from: experts, strangers, the dead, children, secular culture, parents, and enemies. I have written on many subjects—including environmental theology, doubt, deconstruction, theology, sabbath, spiritual formation, liturgy, and desire—but what follows has been born out of the classroom more than any other writing project I've undertaken. Ever watching my students, I've been perplexed, frustrated, and delighted to learn more about them with regard to how they learn, and to discover how when they learn how to learn, the door of faith often swings open for them.

My thesis is simple: Christians should be the most teachable people in the world. They can and should learn from *anyone* and *everyone*. To borrow an obscure line from one of Brighde Mullins's monologues, the Christian should dare say, "Everyone is my teacher."[10]

One

Learning How to Learn

Things had become tight. Our beloved Portland home felt cramped with multiplying roommates, weekend guests, and parish church gatherings. As a result, far too little space remained for the play, exploration, and roughhousing a five-year-old boy like ours required. Our tiny urban lot did not allow us to build out. So my wife, Quinn, quietly planned (I was informed) that we would build *up*. A treehouse!

Our son was ecstatic; I was not.

Building does not come easily to me. Left to myself, I'm inclined toward the life of the mind—books, writing, podcasts, all things intellect. That's my natural environment. "You'd rather *think* about life," a friend once chided me, "than actually live it, wouldn't you?" I blushed in agreement. But there's a historical angle to my disdain for building things. While my own childhood afforded me many skills, learning to work with my hands was not one of them. Mom was a nurse; Dad was a doctor. In my earliest years, they toiled under long work hours as they struggled to keep their marriage intact. These were some of the most painful years of my life. To survive,

I discovered that retreating to the world of reading, thinking, silence, and video games provided a safe haven from my scary world. Dad dragged me outside from time to time, mostly to fish. But learning stereotypical "man things," such as restoring cars, fixing leaky faucets, chopping wood, or building treehouses, wasn't an indigenous part of my childhood landscape.

One of the greatest embarrassments I've faced as I've entered midlife is a lingering shame that I don't know how to do the things I'm "supposed to know how to do" as a man (build things, mostly). The life of the mind has often served as a fig leaf under which I've covered the shame I've had around my masculinity for most of my life. I'm the thinker; my wife is the builder. We've made it work, as long as we agree that I'll be asked to leave my sunless world of thought from time to time to lend muscle holding up a board, find a tool, hammer a nail, or lose a drill bit when needed—the last of which I've all but mastered.

"Can you grab the Phillips screwdriver from the garage?" Quinn asked over her shoulder while hoisting up a four-by-four to the old oak. The first piece of the treehouse was being hung in its place on a bright spring afternoon.

I nodded, heading to the garage just around the corner of our backyard.

Garages terrify me almost as much as building things. They have the feel of a distant land of exotic cultures and unknown tongues. I'm an alien there.

I stood over the toolbox where the screwdrivers were allegedly kept, shuffling about metal items—foreign relics—to locate the requested tool. For two or three minutes, I looked. And looked. And looked. Then, out of nowhere, a surge of emotion welled up within me. And I began to cry.

I have very little to offer by way of explanation. The tears came from nowhere, deep in some chasm in my soul, a mysterious, unexplored cavern in my story.

I sat down.

Why am I crying?

What is happening to me?

Is this a midlife crisis?

Truth was emerging—one of the most consequential epiphanies of my early adulthood. It dawned on me that I didn't know what a Phillips screwdriver looked like. Not a clue. This was something I was supposed to know. A man should know what different screwdrivers look like. But I didn't. A tsunami of shame overcame me. No one had ever taught me what Phillips screwdrivers look like. I was a thirty-five-year-old man unable to do "man stuff." I couldn't hide my ignorance any longer.

Cold tears drying on my cheeks, I returned to Quinn, empty-handed and ashamed. Vulnerably, I named my inadequacy and ignorance and unfulfilled desires that I had for myself as a man. And my inadequacies as a husband. There, in our backyard, I slowly began removing the fig leaf from my hidden shame.

A new chapter was beginning. God wanted to teach me. But he wouldn't do it in any old, normal way. God rarely does. God would do it his way—through the gentle instruction of my wife. She became my teacher. And in so doing, she has helped teach me to be the man God desires. Along the way, I had exposed before my eyes a whole hidden life of sin—pride, arrogance, and fear. All of these would need to be confronted, along with the fear that I could never become the man God wanted me to be. Becoming teachable has a painful but profound way of exposing our most embarrassing insecurities, fears, and idols.

No wonder we're often afraid to be teachable.

Unteachable

Becoming a teachable person has two prerequisites: There must be a teacher and a person willing to be taught. Increasingly, Western culture has become an environment that celebrates and platforms the brilliant teachers. We need teachers. And plenty of resourceful books on teaching can be found at any local bookstore. More elusive, though, are trusted guides showing us how to *become teachable*. Openness to being taught reveals one's hunger for the truth. But it equally reveals one's willingness to embrace their own ignorance as a path toward learning, or what fifteenth-century German Christian bishop Nicholas of Cusa (1401–1464) called "learned ignorance" (Latin, *de docta ignorancia*).[1] Nicholas believed the human mind was incapable of understanding everything—to say nothing of everything about God. Christians, he believed, must begin by first acknowledging their own ignorance. The teachable person names their ignorance. Which is why it is such an elusive virtue—in others and in ourselves. Being teachable is vulnerable business.

Still, there remains little that is closer to the Christian journey than one's willingness to be taught. The very language of *disciple* (Greek, *mathetes*) simply means to be a "learner, pupil, or apprentice." Adjacent to this is the concept of *repentance* (Greek, *metanoia*), which means "to change one's mind." The ancient language used to describe the Christian life is inextricably tied to a life of learning. Sadly, however, learning and repentance are not always qualities Christians are known for—especially in modern America.

What was most surprising in researching this book was my inability to locate one single book dealing with the issue of Christian teachability. Nods are given from time to time. More often, though, I discovered that Christians are commonly perceived in the public square as being the least teachable of our time. True or not, perception is powerful. In 2018, author and historian Timothy Gloege penned a widely circulated article titled "Being Evangelical Means Never Having to Say You're Sorry."[2] Gloege contended that conservative Christians (particularly evangelicals) easily shift blame away from their most embarrassing representatives (particularly in politics) by arguing that they are not truly evangelicals.

Underlying the article is the exposition of the lingering resentment many feel toward evangelicals who appear to many to be unwilling to accept responsibility for their public foibles—along with a further unwillingness to be taught by their failures. Too often, Christians are caricatured as being anti-intellectual,[3] antiscience,[4] and even antiprogress.[5]

If there remains a whiff of merit to these claims, then cultivating teachability will become infinitely important for the church of the twenty-first century. For one, we must be aware that the information age is in its infancy. With the widespread usage of emerging artificial intelligence technologies in the public domain, the quantity of content, information, and knowledge will only proliferate in coming decades. No longer is knowledge scarce or difficult to acquire. This is a gift. But it also presents a new problem. If the primary challenge before the information age was how to acquire knowledge, this new moment will challenge us to discern what knowledge to believe and what to ignore. With information coming at us with such speed as it is, learning how to learn wisely—under the guidance of the Holy Spirit—will be one of the unique qualities of the church.

For another, cultivating teachability will pave a pathway through the power-hungry, politicized, tribal times of today. I recently watched a news segment about a young woman's opening statement in her trial. As a young professional in politics, she had been caught up in a scheme that caused great damage to many. She now faced prison time. As the trial began, she pleaded guilty, publicly confessing that she had failed to listen to the wise people around her. Tears rolled down her face as she named her error before the court. She had been wrong. And she knew it.

I became emotional as I observed a rare cultural moment of humble repentance on national television. That evening, the pundits pounced and mocked the woman for not knowing what *they* had allegedly known all along. They shamed her simply to gain a few political points. Here is the lingering cultural impression one gets from stories like this: The reward for those vulnerable enough to admit their mistakes is to be tarred and feathered— especially if they're on the other side of the political aisle. Rather than celebrate humility, the guilty must be ridiculed for views and clicks. This culture has the graceless habit of demanding repentance while shaming those who risk practicing it.

Teachable people love holding to the truth more than winning an argument. The weaponization of humility I observed that evening has undeniably grotesque consequences for our shared life together—to say nothing of making teachability look like a liability. It has led to a nearly untenable environment where no one is permitted to learn without being publicly mocked. We'd much rather "own the libs" and "own the conservatives" and "own the Christians" and "own the atheists" than behold a beloved creature of God as they are transformed into something a little closer to what God has desired for them. To bolster our own ego, we shame those humble enough to be taught by life's mistakes— all the while hunkering down in increasingly fortified bunkers to guard against being shamed ourselves. Before long, we come to believe that everyone else has some learning to do—except for us.

Barriers to Teachability

At one point or another, we've all humbly submitted ourselves to being taught by someone only to find our own vulnerability weaponized against us. We were demeaned and made to feel inferior, stupid, and worthless for being wrong. Others of us were coerced and manipulated by someone who possessed more knowledge than we did. We were "put in our place." But good teachers don't teach through shame. When we are shaped by shame, we use the same tools on others. Every single semester, I see an aversion in my students to being teachable. For students embarrassed to admit that they came to a Christian university knowing little to nothing about the Bible, they arrive appearing ready to dismiss the whole class. When Christian students from Christian households, who are "supposed" to know Christian things like the Bible, do not know those things, a willingness to learn is perceived as an admission of failure. In their own minds, teachability itself is seen as a defeat.

This is why every single semester, I retell the screwdriver story. And it always hits home. Be it ignorance of screwdrivers or ignorance of the Bible, I often discern in my students a double shame for not knowing something *and* for not knowing something they're "supposed" to know. This twofold assault keeps too many of us from becoming the humble, quiet, and teachable disciples God longs for us to be. Hiding behind the shame of our unformed life, we would rather go on pretending than confess. And in so doing, we are kept from the joy of learning. I must take this into account as a teacher. I have to assume that before I can teach my students the Bible, I must convince them it's okay to be taught—and that I'm a safe person to teach them. They won't be dunked on for their ignorance.

No doubt, teachability exposes the unformed parts of our

lives. For the student, this virtue demands a willingness to submit to someone with more knowledge than they have. And for me—who couldn't identify a Phillips screwdriver—it demanded the humility to learn from a woman what I assumed a man was to know. Teachability is difficult to cultivate, and our lack of teachability reveals the depth of our sin, pride, hard-heartedness, folly, jealousy, and even (in my case) a hidden sexism that presumed that learning from a woman was some kind of problem.

Teachability requires humility before God. And our unteachability exposes our idols. This is why the most teachable people are difficult to identify. They rarely make the news or boast of their brilliance. They don't speak of their accomplishments or broadcast their intellectual prowess. There's no time for public praise. They're too busy quietly, humbly, and gently learning the way of Jesus with hearts hungry to learn. On the other hand, the unteachable can often be the loudest.

I suspect many people fear that being teachable—alongside the intellectual life—will become a slippery slope away from the truth of the gospel. History gives ample reason to fear this. Look at the education system. In 1643, a pamphlet was published that encouraged college students at a major university to a life of robust faith:

> Let every student be plainly instructed, and earnestly pressed, to consider well, [that] the main end of his life and studies is, *to know God and Jesus Christ which is eternal life* (John 17:3) and therefore to lay *Christ* at the bottom, as the only foundation of all sound knowledge and learning.[6]

Which publicly funded university would publish such pious, religious material? Harvard University! Indeed, one of the leading secular institutions of our time began as an institute to train young people for service in God's kingdom. This same story has played out repeatedly. E. Digby Baltzell once argued that of the two hundred universities operating during the Civil War of the 1860s, nearly two-thirds came from Christian pioneers with similar aims as Harvard University's.[7] Were it not for a Christian love of learning, higher education in America as we know it would not exist. In just a few generations, however, what began as spaces in which to explore learning under God's rule and reign have become institutions most opposed to it. In the biting words of the twentieth-century British novelist Dorothy Sayers, "Modern man has kicked down the ladder by which he rose and told his Christian history to go to hell."[8]

As many have experienced, the slippery slope can be real. How many have seen a child or friend lose their faith in college after one class of biology or because of a roommate's influence? Or a spouse abandon their faith because of a podcast—leaving the marriage destroyed. There's a danger in seeking knowledge simply for knowledge's sake. "Beware you be not swallowed up in books," John Wesley wisely wrote. "An ounce of love is worth a pound of knowledge."[9] In fact, the apostle Paul gives much thought to learning in his letters. At one point, Paul warns against the unchecked pursuit of knowledge as the goal: "Knowledge puffs up while love builds up" (1 Corinthians 8:1). In the last days, he writes, the world will be eerily full of those who are "always learning but never able to come to a knowledge of the truth" (2 Timothy 3:7). Indeed, learning and knowledge disconnected from the goal of following Christ can be profoundly destructive. But should we really let a fear of slippery slopes keep us from ever climbing the mountain of truth?

And indeed, nor should we give in to the cultural pressures

we face to look smart. Being informed is not our highest calling. Why is seeking to appear smart so important in our time? Historian Warren Susman has written about the heightened role that performance has played in Western cultures. He calls it a shift from a "culture of character" to a "culture of personality."[10] Who we *are* (in our identity) has become less important than *how* we project ourselves (in our performance) to the world. In line with this shift, individuals are increasingly tempted to replace the call to *be* good with merely *appearing* good. Sociologist Elisabeth Lasch-Quinn pointedly writes, "Performance replaced accomplishment as the path to success. Nebulous qualities such as likeability, uniqueness, and self-confidence edged out duty, right action, and moral courage."[11] Rather than being informed and thoughtful, we would rather *appear* informed and thoughtful.

I experience this temptation to appear well-informed myself. Underneath my discomfort with being taught by another person lies a twisted desire to appear to those in front of me as put together, intellectual, and smart. I don't want to be taught by another person. It demolishes my idol of looking self-taught and self-made. Which is why the information age has become so dangerous for people like me. In a world where I want to appear prodigious and informed as I preach, teach, and speak, I've got a world of digital knowledge from which I can surreptitiously draw. I want the power that comes with knowledge, but not the humility required to receive it. Reading, listening to podcasts, and searching the internet are the ways I can raid from others in quiet so I can project brilliance in public. I'm not always wise. But I have all the tools I need to at least *look* wise.

This temptation to lord one's knowledge over others is nothing new. Jesus teaches his disciples to step away from a similar temptation:

"You know that those who are regarded as rulers of the Gentiles lord it over them, and their high officials exercise authority over them. Not so with you. Instead, whoever wants to become great among you must be your servant, and whoever wants to be first must be slave of all. For even the Son of Man did not come to be served, but to serve, and to give his life as a ransom for many." (Mark 10:42–45)

Jesus, here, flips the script on what had become normative in his own day. The disciples wanted seats of honor. They wanted to look important and powerful. Anyone who loves God is prone to embodying this kind of pride.[12] They can be tempted to want to be seen and known as right, honorable, and excellent. Like the disciples of Jesus' day, we have a proclivity to be ahead; to lead; to get attention, power, dominance; and to curry importance. And like the disciples, we must be corrected. The disciple is not called to "be right." In fact, this quality is entirely omitted from the fruit of the Spirit passage of Galatians 5. This is no mistake. Our task is not showing that we are leading the way; the task is following the Son of Man. The journey of Jesus is not a power grab or exercise in reputation management. The journey is the journey down—to humble Christlikeness.

Teachability in Scripture

Scripture repeatedly invites us to cultivate a posture of teachability to receive wisdom and understanding. We see this in Solomon, who is described as possessing a wisdom that was "greater than the wisdom of all the people of the East" (1 Kings 4:30). Solomon's wisdom and knowledge were so widely known that "his fame spread to all the surrounding nations. He spoke three thousand proverbs and his songs numbered a thousand and five. He spoke about plant life, from the cedar of Lebanon to the hyssop that grows out of walls. He also spoke about animals and birds, reptiles and fish. From all nations people came to listen to Solomon's wisdom, sent by all the kings of the world, who had heard of his wisdom" (vv. 31–34). While the Old Testament contains only a few of his proverbs, Solomon is said to have written thousands of poems about life—about *all* of life. Wisdom, at least the kind Solomon had, goes outside the lines of even spiritual truth. Wisdom is truth for *all* of life.

In addition, the proverbs repeatedly envision holy living as a humble submission to the teachings of the wise. Many proverbs record the words of a wise father to a maturing son: "Listen, my son, to your father's instruction and do not forsake your mother's teaching" (Proverbs 1:8). The "wise" person is even distinguished from the "fool" by their capacity to be taught. Unlike the fool, a wise person is correctable—always ready to learn more. "Whoever loves discipline loves knowledge," the author reflects, "but whoever hates correction is stupid" (12:1). Even economic and social flourishing are tied to one's teachability: "Poverty and disgrace come to him who ignores instruction, but whoever heeds reproof is honored" (13:18 ESV). Wisdom, in these texts, is less something one has; it is who someone is. "Give instruction to a wise man, and he will be still wiser; teach a righteous man, and he will increase in learning" (9:9 ESV).

The crown of the wise is a teachable spirit. As Old Testament professor Daniel Estes writes, these twin virtues of wisdom and teachability are biblically indistinguishable:

The teachable person learns from past tradition. Rather than demanding the right to learn solely from personal experience, an approach to life fraught with risk, he acquires wise counsel from those who have preceded him. Eschewing total indepen- dence of judgment, the wise person learns as well from the accumulated insights of others.[13]

Teachability would stand out as a distinctive of the early Jesus community. We see this in what has been called the Great Commission in the final chapter of Matthew's gospel. Jesus has been teaching his disciples for three years. And now they will go and teach the world. Jesus outlines their marching orders:

> "Therefore go and make disciples of all nations, baptizing them in the name of the Father and of the Son and of the Holy Spirit, and teaching them to obey everything I have commanded you. And surely I am with you always, to the very end of the age." (Matthew 28:19–20)

The ministry of teaching and the making of disciples—in the moral and missional vision of Jesus—are intimately intertwined with one another. To be taught is to be a disciple. And to be a disciple is to teach.[14] Most importantly, the ability to teach rightly first means being taught rightly. The capacity for these individ- uals to go into the world and teach the way of Jesus *assumes* that they have spent the necessary time being taught the way of Jesus.

This vision shaped the early church. Spirit-formed leaders, Paul later wrote, should be "able to teach" (1 Timothy 3:2; 2 Timothy 2:24). But the biblical writer James warns against becoming teachers too quickly (James 3:1–12). Paul further commands newer Christians to wait before leading or teaching (1 Timothy 3:6). The early church desperately needed teachers, but the process by which they could do so demanded a lengthy process of submission, humility, and character formation. Before these leaders could teach, they had to show themselves to be teachable.

Writing to Timothy, Paul describes this kind of culture: "Do not rebuke an older man harshly, but exhort him as if he were your father. Treat younger men as brothers, older women as mothers, and younger women as sisters, with absolute purity" (1 Timothy 5:1–2). In Christ, everyone was to see others as their equals or as teachers. No one was to be looked down on. Not every Christian was to teach. But every Christian was to be teachable.

This led to a countercultural community unlike anything the world had seen. Look at the case of Apollos, a "learned man, with a thorough knowledge of the Scriptures" (Acts 18:24). Scripture holds no hesitancy in portraying a man being taught by a married couple—Priscilla (the wife) and Aquila (the husband). Such an arrangement subverted nearly every established norm of social life in the Roman Empire, as would have Paul's command regarding women. "A woman," Paul writes, "should learn in quietness and full submission" (1 Timothy 2:11). For modern readers, this sounds offensive, macho, or downright sexist. But for Paul, this command was delivered in an ancient context where women weren't permitted to learn or afforded formal education. Paul wasn't limiting women; Paul was liberating women. In a culture that stifled the intellectual pursuits of females, Paul *commands* them to embrace a life of learning. No wonder Rome perceived these Christians to be so threatening. They let their women read. And they shamelessly hung their sacred story of a resurrected Lord on the lips of the women on that first Easter morning (John 20).

The learning would not yet be complete. Just as Jesus prepared to ascend to heaven, he told his disciples a soon-coming teacher would continue teaching them, just as Jesus had. This Holy Spirit "will teach you all things and will remind you of everything I have said to you" (John 14:26). Later, Jesus told them this Spirit "will guide you into all the truth" (16:13). The Greek indicative mood (the mood of reality or certainty) in these statements are instructive. The Spirit would lead these disciples into "all things" and "all the truth." Jesus, here, is describing the Spirit as our master teacher—a Spirit dwelling in all who follow Christ. This teacher does not teach merely "Christian" truths. There are no "Christian" truths. Nor are there "secular" truths. There is only truth. And all truth is God's truth.[15] As Augustine later reflected, "Let every good and true Christian understand that wherever truth may be found, it belongs to his Master."[16] This would be codified later in the church by saints such as Ambrose and Thomas Aquinas, who would say the phrase *omne verum, a quocumque dicatur, a Spiritu Sancto est*: "Every true thing, no matter who says it, is from the Holy Spirit."[17]

Teachability in Christian History

The spirit of teachability is evidenced throughout Christian history. In *Destroyer of the gods*, New Testament scholar Larry Hurtado explores how early Christian communities shared a commitment to the sacred written Scriptures.[18] After the time of the apostles, the need to protect, copy, and disseminate their precious writings became uniquely pressing. The apostles' stories needed a community to guard them and pass them along. With its early adoption of writing and reading as a preferred medium for divine revelation, the infant church soon became (intentionally or not) a community of writers, readers, and learners.

Given that only about 10 to 15 percent of Roman society could read or write, the earliest Christians emerged as some of the most intellectually savvy people in the Roman world.[19] Paul's command to Timothy to "devote yourself to the public reading of Scripture" (1 Timothy 4:13) assumes that the church *should* be capable of reading out loud.[20] Becoming a Christian placed a person in the middle of one of the most radical learning communities the world has ever seen. No wonder the Roman ruler Festus declared to Paul, "Your great learning is driving you insane" (Acts 26:24).

This hunger for learning is evident in the writings of early church fathers such as Irenaeus, Tertullian, Cyprian, and Augustine. When we read their surviving writings, we discover a community of pastors and scholars who opted to lead the Christian community with a simultaneous commitment to Scripture *and* the best learning from the surrounding Roman world. Quoting philosophers, historians, and detractors, these early Christian minds raised their heads high in the intellectual climate of their time. An entire community of thinkers known as the "apologists" set their minds to engaging that climate by defending the truth of Jesus. They possessed a humble knowledge. Many of these writers ended their theological careers publicly acknowledging the things that they had discovered that were wrong in their own thinking. For instance, Augustine's *The Retractations* reflects a spirit of humility and teachability as to what he had been wrong about.[21]

Soon, Celtic monasteries would emerge as places of learning. Known as *muintir*, these "colonies of heaven" served as interlocking communities of respite, prayer, justice, creativity, and, most notably, education. As Celtic Christianity spread throughout the British Isles, so did its transformative educational system. This was, in the words of Ian Bradley's *The Celtic Way*, "a combination of commune, retreat house, mission station, hotel, hospital, school, university, arts centre and power-house for the local community—a source not only of spiritual energy but also of hospitality, learning and cultural enlightenment."[22] As the gospel of Jesus spread, so did a new and revolutionary form of Christian education where discipleship and intellectual formation were joined at the hip.

In the medieval church, Charlemagne (747–814 CE), the king of the Franks, was inspired by Augustine to see that a nation could be discipled through education. Considered by some to be the patron saint of scholarship, Charlemagne formed a school in which his own children could be educated. He had a library that may have outdone any of his time. In fact, the only surviving literature from his life is that which was written by monks as directed by his hand. Cathedrals and monasteries established schools in which the children of nearby nobles could be educated. Charlemagne was so convinced that the leaders of the church should be teachable that he is said to have sent investigators to find any priest or monk unwilling to learn and have them released from their clerical duties. As one biographer notes, "Education was . . . carefully tended. The partially illiterate [Charlemagne] believed that success in his political and religious reforms depended on learning: 'although doing right is better than knowledge, knowledge comes before doing.'"[23]

The spirit of learning further fueled the Protestant Reformation—at least in part. Before the time of Martin Luther, the writings of the New Testament were only broadly known in the West through Latin translations. But due to the intellectual renewal brought about by Erasmus, Europe increasingly returned to the study of classic languages. With this came an increased desire to see the Bible translated into everyday tongues. Soon after Luther's encounter with the writings of Paul and the gospel, he set on a path to make the Scriptures available to all and to complete a full copy of the Bible in German. All of this, no doubt, was possible because of Luther's education and insight. As Gene Veith wrote, "Luther was in touch with this new scholarship and was a master of Greek, as well as of his own German language. He also depended upon his colleague Melanchthon, the notable Hebrew scholar and classical educator."[24] The Protestant Reformation, which brought fulfillment to the desire to read the Bible in everyday language, was at the same time a renewal of the way people of faith could and did learn.

Learning led to the Reformation. And learning went wherever the Reformation went. Luther understood that the future of the movement depended on an educated people who could read Scripture rightly. In line with this, he believed schools should be established throughout Germany that would teach the Bible—but not just the Bible. Luther saw a well-rounded education as a part of Christian discipleship. In 1524, he wrote a treatise titled "To the Councilmen of All Cities in Germany That They Establish and Maintain Christian Schools."[25] The document lit a fire of interest in public education. German cities, Luther believed, should be supported by compulsory schools where the young were formed in the ways of Christ as they learned standardized skills of math, science, and languages. His influence led to the formation of a Protestant university in Wittenberg that would become a model for others to come.[26] Luther's renewals retrieved the gospel message—and inalterably changed how people learned.

The mantle would be picked up by John Calvin, who believed

that part of the "yoke" of following Jesus Christ was learning. "Take my yoke upon you," Jesus commands, "and learn from me" (Matthew 11:29). Discipleship and learning, for Calvin, were synonymous. He spoke of the necessity for the Christian to cultivate what he called "a teachable spirit."[27] Without being teachable, we will learn nothing from Christ. In one sermon on Deuteronomy 10, Calvin points out that God commands Moses to chisel out two stone tablets on which to write down the commandments. Calvin then explains that Moses had to bring the tablets *up* the mountain. "Then I came back down the mountain and put the tablets in the ark I had made, as the LORD commanded me, and they are there now" (Deuteronomy 10:5). This little story inspired Calvin's theology of learning. To love God was to bring to God a heart and mind ready to be taught.[28] Human nature may be (in Calvin's words) "obstinate and opinionated," but the gospel frees us to learn and be taught by a God who writes on our hard hearts.[29]

Everywhere Calvinism (the movement inspired by Calvin's teachings) went, learning seemed to follow. These reformations led to the establishment of countless universities and houses of learning.[30] Cornelius Plantinga unpacks why this happened:

> Why such enthusiasm for Christian colleges among Calvinists? No doubt one reason is that John Calvin himself loved the life of learning. Calvin understood that God created human beings to hunt and gather truth, and that, as a matter of fact, the capacity for doing so amounts to one feature of the image of God in them (Col. 3:10). So Calvin fed on knowledge as gladly as a deer on sweet corn.[31]

Because Calvin fused the life of the mind with Christian faithfulness, education became part of the church's mission. As many historians have pointed out, with the spread of Christianity came the spread of universities. Universities were Christian inventions.[32] And as Christianity spread, so did deep learning and intellectual rigor.

Raising Hands

All of this may surprise some. Not only does the Bible invite us to become people who grow in wisdom and knowledge, but the history of God's people reveals that Christians have often seen learning and discipleship as the same journey. There have been times when this was not the case. But often it is. Following Jesus is the journey to becoming teachable people who have the guiding hand of the Teacher known as the Holy Spirit inside of them.

Consider how John concludes his biography of Jesus. John writes an arresting statement: "Jesus did many other things as well. If every one of them were written down, I suppose that even the whole world would not have room for the books that would be written" (John 21:25). In essence, John is saying, "There's so much more to know!" Christian historian Mark Noll believes this is a model for understanding intellectual life under God's rule and reign:

> What is true for the life and work of Christ . . . is also true for the life of the mind. If the meaning of what Jesus did and is exceeds the capacity of all the books that could be written, so too the meaning of what Jesus did and is, with respect only to the intellectual life, exceeds the capacity of all the books that could ever be written. Christian believers who realize that it is impossible ever to fathom the depths of wisdom and

knowledge hidden in Jesus Christ nonetheless know that the proper place to begin serious intellectual labor is the same place where we begin all other serious enterprises . . . the revelation of God in Jesus Christ.[33]

If this is true, then following Jesus should be the most enlivening, challenging, vivifying, and fulfilling lifelong continuing education anyone could dream of. There's *always* more to learn. Loving Jesus is the same as loving the truth. To seek the truth, one must seek Christ. Because in Christ, all truth is hidden. There, then, is no more demonstrable way to express our love for God than in a desire to want to know and understand more about him. Loving God and desiring knowledge of God are inseparable. "We cannot love God," writes Alister McGrath, "without wanting to understand more of him."[34]

I have a colleague named Dr. Melisa Ortiz Berry—a luminary expert on ancient and contemporary church history. Students love her. Melisa tells me of a time when she was a child and walked into a church service with her cousin. Having only ever been in a Catholic or Baptist church, she saw something she had never seen before—Christians raising their hands. Turning to her cousin, she asked, "Do they have questions?" As would any child, she saw the world through her experience—the classroom. What looked to her like people with questions was really a community loving God.

Melisa's story stuck with me. Isn't it interesting that the thing someone does to worship God in church is the same thing someone does in a classroom to ask a question? A fitting image, indeed. What if good questions are a sign of true worship?

The treehouse eventually got built. And I can safely say now that I know what a Phillips screwdriver looks like. As I humbled myself to learn from my wife, I was being formed in myself, and I was allowing her to give me *her* gift. The experience formed both of us. Being teachable shapes us. But it also gives others the gift of sharing out of their own lives. "A teachable life," writes biblical scholar Donald Guthrie, "is a life lived in wholehearted response to God's kind provision *for the sake of others*."[35]

To be teachable, then, is to allow someone else to love you.

Two

Learning from Experts

Three people wrote the majority of the New Testament: Paul, John, and Luke. As a percentage of total word count, John wrote approximately 20 percent, Paul wrote 23 percent, and Luke wrote an astonishing 27.5 percent. Much is known about Paul and John. But Luke remains largely enigmatic. He is only mentioned three times in the entire New Testament (Colossians 4:14; 2 Timothy 4:11; Philemon 24). Still, despite scant information about him, some details emerge.

What do we know about him? Luke was likely a Gentile. If true, this provides insight into how the earliest Christian community took shape. Before the messianic movement of Jesus, Jews and Gentiles were ideologically, culturally, and religiously at odds. Gentiles despised the Jews. Jews considered Gentiles dirty and ungodly. If Luke was one, we should be amazed by the fact that a Gentile would be given so much literary acreage in the New Testament. That the earliest Christian community (predominantly composed of Jewish followers of Jesus) would willingly entrust *their* testimony about *their* Messiah into the hands of a Gentile speaks volumes about the impact of the gospel in early Christianity. Clearly, the centuries-old wall of ethnic hostility between Jews and Gentiles was crumbling because of the story of Jesus. Healing was happening.

Luke is also described as an investigator (Luke 1:3) of the Jesus story. More importantly, he sees his task as handing down what the first eyewitnesses experienced and taught about Jesus (v. 2). This means Luke likely wasn't one of the original disciples of Jesus. In his description of his call, something about his occupation rises to the surface. Luke's word for eyewitness is *autoptes*. Look closely. Notice a connection to English? Luke is not merely passing on an eyewitness account; he's doing an *autopsy* (a derivation of the Greek word). Who would use a word like this?

Luke is a doctor. Paul explicitly calls him the "beloved physician" (Colossians 4:14 ESV). This helps us sort out why Luke tells his story about Jesus the way he did. As in contemporary times, ancient doctors would undergo years of rigorous training under an established physician—learning, observing, and honing their craft. This level of training not only prepared Luke to tell his account about Jesus, but it also shaped his message. His trained medical eye saw things others overlooked. It's no surprise, then, to discover that Luke recounts more healing stories than any other gospel writer. Luke sees Jesus through the lens of his day job.

The doctor is in.

Luke's story taps into a broad theme linking many of the biblical authors and characters—namely, that a disproportionate number of them were experts in their world. No other ancient religious anthology boasts so diverse a set of authors as the Bible. Over its three thousand years of composition history, texts and stories came from kings (David and Solomon), shepherds (Moses and Amos), theologians (Paul), royal priests (Jeremiah and

Ezekiel), soldiers (Joshua), tax collectors (Matthew), fishermen (Peter and John), scribes (Ezra), and even cupbearers (Nehemiah). These were, in many cases, people in power with great influence. God, of course, uses the lowly and the foolish to reveal himself to the world (1 Corinthians 1:27), but he also uses the high and the wise. As such, the voices of Scripture represent a wide array of people from different ethnicities, cultures, and socioeconomic backgrounds—many of whom were considered experts in their world. Reading biblical literature, then, is submitting to a series of expert witnesses about the God of the universe.

Furthermore, many of these individuals came from environments that were considered the intellectual centers of antiquity. Consider the following: Abraham was raised in Ur, where the most extensive ancient library was discovered. Daniel resided in Babylon, receiving a privileged Babylonian education (Daniel 1). Moses was "instructed in all the wisdom of the Egyptians" (Acts 7:22 ESV), receiving a first-rate education in Pharaoh's household. Paul's hometown of Tarsus boasted one of the leading ancient universities of the day. Paul even studied under *the* leading Bible expert of his day, being "educated at the feet of Gamaliel" (Acts 22:3 ESV). Apollos—said to be a "learned man" with a deep knowledge of Scripture—was raised near Alexandria with its now lost wonder of the world, the great Alexandrian library (Acts 18:24).[1]

These biblical texts, which have nurtured Christian faith for centuries, were in most cases written by experts. That's to say nothing of the expert class of "scribes" whose assignment to copy and disseminate the text made it available for the next generation. This reveals an important truth: Even the writing of inspired Scripture reveals God's contentment with using expert skills of human writing, reading, and thinking to accomplish his purposes. Isn't this one of the first lessons Israel learned after liberation from Egypt?

In Exodus 31, God used the finely honed artisan skills of Bezalel and Oholiab to build the tabernacle. Reading carefully, we see that God used their *existing* skills. On these empowered creatives, theologian Jack Levison writes, "God tops them up with the spirit, not to learn new skills, but to teach the ones they have already mastered through a lifetime of learning and practice."[2] No doubt, developing the skills necessary to build something like the tabernacle would take a lifetime. Grace, it seems, uses human sweat equity.

We quickly pop off the quip that God "trains the called." Sometimes. But not always. Other times, God "calls the trained." Experts also play their part in God's economy.

Which brings us back to Luke. Christians sometimes live in a standoffish relationship with the experts of our own time. This chapter won't argue that the Christian should defer to or accept *everything* the expert says. Experts can be wrong. But too often experts are dismissed out of fear—a fear that they seek to rob us of our faith, have knowledge that could challenge our church, or desire to use their knowledge as a power play. Some have even gone so far as to caricature listening to experts as the sign that one does not believe in God or trust in Jesus.

Two extremes tend to emerge. Some reject expert advice in its entirety; others uncritically accept everything experts say without humbly acknowledging that experts have the capacity to be wrong. The result, sadly, is an unprecedented division of relationship and a sundering of Christian unity around misconceptions of how to learn from the expert.

Misunderstanding the role of an expert can be deadly business. Years ago, a young man in my circle came under the influence of a faith-healing ministry. I knew there was a problem when he started getting flu symptoms. In his new community, he was being taught that going to a doctor signaled a lack of trust in God. Fearing for his health, I had a come-to-Jesus conversation with him. I pointed out that the very Christ follower who teaches us the most about the healing power of the Holy Spirit in the books of Luke and Acts was a doctor. I asked him, "Did ancient people lack faith by going to Luke to hear about Jesus, the Great Physician?" The young man soon decided to see a doctor and received some much-needed medicine. This experience taught me that a thoughtful Christian theology around expertise isn't merely needed; it can save lives. If God is our healer, we've got little business limiting his sovereign means of healing.

What Is an Expert?

Our moment in history feels almost euphoric. The vast flood of knowledge and information available to nearly everyone has altered the human experience in unparalleled ways. Knowledge is good. But it can also be dangerous. When people have access to endless knowledge, it becomes difficult to discern the difference between experts and those who simply have access to expert knowledge. That is, we begin equating one's ability to acquire knowledge with being knowledgeable. This scenario has made us simultaneously prone to undercompetence and overconfidence. Researchers have called this the Dunning-Kruger effect. The subjects in their studies often had a cognitive bias to believe very strongly things they knew very little about. Think about that person in your life who seems dead set on their knowledge—showing time and again that their folly gets the best of them. One's confidence, it turns out, has little to no connection to competence.[3]

This exposes a crucial lesson—naivete often blinds us. I've experienced this firsthand. I first studied *koine* Greek in college. Learning the language of the New Testament entirely reshaped the way I read Scripture. My knowledge grew by the day. But sadly, overconfidence followed close behind. I noticed that being able to read just a little of the original biblical languages—combined with endless access to lexicons and word studies—simultaneously expanded my knowledge *and* my arrogance. My newfound ability to identify a few Greek words and grammatical constructions seemed to give me permission to believe that *my* interpretation of the Bible was right. Rather than humbling me, this new knowledge, borrowing a phrase from Paul, "puffed up" my mind (1 Corinthians 8:1). I started quoting Greek in my sermons not to serve the people I was preaching to but to buttress my own flimsy ego.

I've since continued studying Greek. But I grieve the ways I abused these skills to leverage power and influence. I learned a valuable lesson: Having a little expert knowledge doesn't make someone an expert. In fact, it often makes someone dangerous. We are often overconfident in things we are undercompetent in.

Confidence is good—as long as it's in the right things. Luke describes the crowd's impression of the first apostles at Pentecost: "When they saw the *courage* of Peter and John and realized that they were unschooled, ordinary men, they were astonished and they took note that these men had been with Jesus" (Acts 4:13, italics mine). Their courage drew in the crowds. What's important, of course, is that the apostles' confidence did not lie in expert knowledge; their courage came because "these men had been with Jesus." Christian confidence, as such, is proportional to one's intimacy with Christ.

Sadly, the Dunning-Kruger effect is often on full display whenever someone confidently makes a declaration about something they aren't competent to speak on. We see this when a religious leader pontificates whether someone should or shouldn't get a vaccine, despite having never cracked open a medical textbook or gone to medical school. Or when a critic of the Christian faith rails on and on against Christians for stupidly believing in a Bible they've self-determined to be sexist, patriarchal, and homophobic—all without ever having done the hard work of listening to the community of biblical scholars who have devoted their lives to interpreting said texts. Or when an activist who has never taken a single class on constitutional or legal theory argues that America should do away with the democratic system because it does not fit their own ideological proclivities.

It's tempting to rush quickly into anointing oneself an expert. But in so doing, we fail to receive the gifts of knowledge God has so graciously given to others. This is why we *must* define an expert in our particular moment—everyone thinks they are one.

An expert is someone who through hard work, study, and perseverance has earned a weight of authority in a particular domain of knowledge or activity. This takes time and great energy. One researcher, Anders Ericsson, famously argued that expertise is only possible for someone who has given ten years or ten thousand hours to developing their skill.[4] Similarly, scholar Howard Gardner examined the lives of Einstein, Picasso, Stravinsky, and Gandhi in his book *Creating Minds*. Gardner made the convincing case that those who most impacted human culture with their own expertise did so because of long, difficult, and painful struggles of preparation. Biological or genetic factors were not the driving forces. In short, no one is born an expert.[5]

Expertise comes from sweat, not genetics. There are prodigies, no doubt. But they are the exception, not the rule.

Now, an astute reader will notice a problem with my definition. What gives me the authority to define what an expert is? Interestingly, the study of expertise is an actual area of expertise. Perhaps no one has written more extensively on the topic than Roger Kneebone. In his book *Expert*, Kneebone unpacks what he learned after a career of studying experts. One vexing problem, Kneebone admits, is that true expertise is almost always impossible to identify. To do so is challenging (Kneebone calls it a "tall order"), even for someone who has spent his academic career studying experts in their field, their mastery in their discipline, their development of intuition and judgment, and their insights into how they learned to learn. The difficulty lies in the simple reality that true experts don't seek fame, celebrity, or power for their knowledge. A true expert does not just master their knowledge; they are mastered by it. Expertise, he writes, "is the art that conceals art."[6]

Kneebone identifies an important distinction. He differentiates between the one who *has* expertise and someone who *is* an expert. Anyone can have expertise on anything. This is the kind of knowledge everyone can (and should) seek. But the road to becoming an expert is different. It requires traveling through many stages—from novice to advanced beginner, competence, proficiency, and then expertise.[7] Anyone can pursue expertise in any domain. We all can learn how motors work, why fish swim upstream, or what carbohydrates are made of. But *being* an expert is something different. An expert has something Michael Polanyi called "tacit" knowledge[8] and Dallas Willard called "knowledge by acquaintance."[9] An expert does not merely know *about* things. At the cost of great time, struggle, toil, sacrifice, and accountability, they know personally and intimately the objects of their study. Put another way, anyone can have expertise and be wrong. But an expert can lose their job for being wrong.

This distinction doesn't mean nonexperts should be disqualified from speaking on a given subject. Anyone can and should speak freely about anything. But there is a difference, Kneebone argues, between what he calls "interactional expertise" and "contributory expertise."[10] Interactional expertise is anyone's capacity to interact with and dialogue with experts in a particular field. Contributory expertise, however, is one's ability to *contribute* to that body of expert knowledge. We all should strive for interactional expertise, growing in knowledge of subjects ranging from language to biblical studies, gardening, and at-home medicine. But we must remain humble and clear. Simply being able to speak about a topic does not mean we are experts in that topic.

Consider a parable. Imagine an asteroid is discovered to be careening toward a catastrophic collision with earth in one week's time. One option for survival remains. If set in motion, a perfectly aimed atomic weapon could divert the asteroid from its path and save earth. However, there is just one office space with one hundred seats where the experts can hatch a plan. In that moment, we recognize the importance of certain expertise. What everyone needs—the whole world, in fact—are experts in their given fields (astrophysics, astronomy, nuclear physics, and more) to drop everything they're doing and get together to determine a plan. The last thing we want the experts doing is spending precious hours scrolling through Facebook and reading about the fears and anxieties of friends and family. In many cases, an expert's work can either save or kill. Again, I'm a theologian. I believe in my craft. My work is important. But I'll be the first to say there's no need whatsoever for a professional theologian to take up one of those seats in that office space.

Wisdom includes being able to identify who is and who is not an expert in a particular area. Claiming to be an expert without being one borders on sin—the bearing of false witness (Exodus 20:16 ESV), which God passionately forbids. If we do not learn how to acknowledge one's limits, we merely reflect the culture around us that uncritically and furiously exalts equality, assuming every idea and opinion is equal in value. The result—as Tom Nichols prophetically explores in *The Death of Expertise*—is a culture that cannot recognize the truth that hits them in the face.[11] In a social media matrix that amplifies all voices, the voice of the quiet, wise expert is lost in the chaotic chatter. I should not wish a carpenter, barista, or theologian to be responsible to stop that approaching asteroid. Nor do I think an atheist like Richard Dawkins has expert knowledge in matters of religion or theology (which he often, ironically, claims to have). No, we need to listen to the right people for the right things.

Fearing Experts

Admittedly, there's good reason to fear experts. They can correct us. Early in my teaching career, an opportunity to teach a coveted course on church history presented itself at the seminary I had attended. At the semester's midpoint, we were covering the life and theology of John Wesley. I arranged to have Dr. Larry Shelton—our resident Wesley scholar—deliver a couple of lectures. His expertise on Wesley is second to few. The class was elated that he agreed to join us. I lectured on Wesley's story. And Shelton lectured on Wesley's theology. After my talks,

Shelton got up and waxed eloquent, dancing through an extant knowledge of Wesley's thought. He never even used notes. I was blushing inside. I got to teach alongside a hero. I was, apparently, one of the experts now.

Following class, Shelton invited me to his office. Excited that he was going to affirm my work, I made my way to his backroom study. He shared a few pleasant affirmations. Then he came to his point. "You totally missed it, A.J.," he said. "You missed a whole section of Wesley's life." I was so caught off guard that the breath in my lungs seemed to be sucked out of my body. He showed me how I had overlooked some of the more integral aspects of Wesley's upbringing—to say nothing of getting Wesley's birth date wrong. Sensing my deflation, he shared about the life a teacher lives: "Part of being a teacher," he reminded me, "is being accountable to others for what you teach." Correction was part of the territory. And if I wanted the privilege of teaching the truth, I had better be ready to be shattered by it from time to time.

The power of the expert is that they have knowledge and insight that may humble us. But the teachable Christian resists a fear of truth and knowledge. When we are afraid of knowledge, we become like the shop teacher who refused to enroll in a continuing education course. Why? The shop teacher may find out things he has been wrong about. In learning something new, he'd have to change the way he taught his course.[12] We can cower with a similar fear that being taught means having to rethink and reshape life. And it is true. To learn implies a willingness to change. In a quiet effort to not have to change or rethink our ideas, we insulate ourselves from those who may know more than we do. But what is Christian discipleship but a never-ending journey of ongoing education?[13] Dallas Willard once lamented that these fears are what keep so many from taking Christianity seriously. For many, Willard believed, becoming a Christian can lead to an unwillingness to learn from others. Too soon, the church becomes an "intellectual slum."[14]

Living in fear of knowledge leads to an anti-intellectualism that cuts off the journey of learning. Where would this fear—and anti-intellectualism—come from? In his book *The Scandal of the Evangelical Mind*, Mark Noll traces the history of revivalism that swept American college campuses in the 1800s and illustrates their tendency to emphasize emotionalism over rationalism, placing, to some extent, the heart *over* the head.[15] A lasting consequence of this was a growing disdain for higher education in much of conservative Christianity.

Others have argued that the very impulse behind fundamentalism is simultaneously a desire to want to change the world and a fear of being tainted by it. In her book *Apostles of Reason*, Molly Worthen has shown how early American evangelicals held a dual commitment to fearing the world and wanting to change it. This led to a sectarian mindset in Christian Bible colleges and universities that pulled away from the world to "preserve" the truth.[16] The result, as Os Guinness writes, is an "anti-intellectualism [that] is a disposition to discount the importance of truth and the life of the mind. Living in a sensuous culture and increasingly emotional democracy, American evangelicals in the last generation have simultaneously toned up their bodies and dumbed down their minds."[17]

Even if unfounded, these proclivities to pull away from the world make sense to me. During my own doctoral research, I studied a biblical theology of creation. This meant devouring stacks and stacks of books and articles on climate change and ecological degradation in a dark British library. In doing so, I discovered how few outspoken Christians worked in these environmental fields.[18] The result was that I had to submit much of my ecological research to the knowledge of those outside the Christian faith—as though this were a problem. What this exposed in me was a hidden assumption that the church *should* be leading the ecological conversation. How many times have I heard someone say, "The church should be leading the climate crisis. We should be the ones out front on this"?

While getting Christians into every field is critical, I found myself agitated at the assumption that Christians should have to lead a conversation to be able to learn from it. The message the church often sends the world is that we are only willing to learn when we are the ones in the front. Rather, we should be capable, humble learners who are being transformed "with ever-increasing glory" into the image of Christ.[19] In a world where nobody listens, perhaps our very mission begins with listening.

Some will respond by asking, "If we have the Bible, tradition, the Holy Spirit, and the gospel of grace, why should we need an expert?" In the early to mid-1900s, a German theologian named Paul Tillich took up this very question. For Tillich, if the church did not believe that God could use the world to teach it, then it would cultivate a dangerous worldview that would cut the church off from learning and correction. The church is a prophet to the world, to be sure. But, for Tillich, sometimes the world was a prophet to the church. His term for this was "reverse prophetism."[20] Tillich believed the church could be sanctified by the corrective knowledge of the world. The world was to be understood as the community that could correct God's people from time to time.

Does Tillich's idea hold up to Scripture? An answer requires great wisdom. "Do not love the world or anything in the world," the apostle John warns us, "[for] if anyone loves the world, love for the Father is not in them" (1 John 2:15). No question, a Christian should live discerningly in this world and recognize that the enemy of God is at work. But there's a balance. The same Bible that urges us to be discerning is the same book that tells us God moved the heart of the pagan King Cyrus to allow the exiled Jews to return and rebuild the temple and sent King Nebuchadnezzar to teach Israel and Judah humility. In Scripture, God often uses outsiders to teach insiders important lessons. To believe in God's sovereignty, indeed, is to accept a dynamic view of the world as an environment where God generously gives gifts of intellect and insights where he wills it.

Which means that when Jonas Salk discovered a cure for polio in 1955, he didn't do so as a confessing Christian. Raised in a family of Orthodox Jewish-Russian immigrants, Salk never claimed a concrete commitment to any faith tradition. Does that mean his work is no gift from God? Indeed, the mind of Jonas Salk was a gift from God—the vessel for the ideas that saved millions of lives. I confess that I disagree with much of Tillich's theology. But I wholeheartedly agree that a Christian should be able to identify the gifts of God wherever God has given them, whether inside or outside the church.

The church can both teach the world and learn from the world because there are no two kinds of truth. No such thing exists as "biblical truth" and "expert truth.[21] There's one truth. Nothing more. The church should be committed, first and foremost, to the faithful witness of Scripture. But this dogged faithfulness to biblical truth should never preclude her from listening carefully to the neuroscientist, biologist, or astrophysicist whose work may help them see more clearly the world God has made. Listening to the expert—in this context—becomes part of the church's witness to the world. Just as the apostle Philip climbed into the Ethiopian eunuch's cart to listen and eventually bring the good news to him, we too can enter the world of experts and listen so we might speak truth and be sanctified in our call.[22] Should we really expect the world to listen to our witness if we're unwilling to listen to it?

Using Experts Well

So how do we learn from experts? We do ourselves (and others) a profound disservice by uncritically using experts without love and wisdom. When I read the insights of an expert in my own research and writing, I do so with some assumptions. Consider the following five general rules for being taught by the expert:

1. Not Everyone Is an Expert

Wisdom includes acknowledging the boundaries of expertise. An expert, for example, is not an expert because of excitement about a topic. The ability to arouse emotion doesn't qualify someone as an expert. In other words, zeal and truthfulness aren't synonyms. Nor does having read a blog post, composed a witty series of social media posts, or binge-watched an array of YouTube videos lend authority in a domain. Social status and wealth have little connection to expertise. Being a billionaire does not make someone wise. In a world where money talks, we belittle the truth when we assume that one's knowledge of medicine, eschatology, or climate change is directly tied to the size of their hedge fund. Nor are the chances that someone is an expert heightened by the size of their following. Celebrity means nothing to wisdom—whether referring to those in power or those with massive followings on Instagram, TikTok, or X.

2. "The Experts" Aren't a Thing

Many writers try to gain authority by quoting experts. We hear it often: "Experts say . . ." Or, "Scholars say . . ." Or "Science says . . ." The way this is phrased assumes there exists some community that stands together, arms locked, in uniform agreement about a topic. In the realm of logic, this has been called the logical fallacy of the "false universal."[23]

The use of false universals is common and seductive. We all do it. Often, in place of good argument, we rely on some mythic community of experts who articulate what we ourselves have failed to argue convincingly. This is endemic in Christian culture. How often do we say, "The Bible says . . ."? I catch myself often saying, "The commentators say . . ." as though they're in agreement. Sadly, what often follows "the Bible says" is insidious and shallow. We use "the Bible says" to baptize whatever we say. I once heard a biblical scholar explain that she would not allow students in her classes to ever use the phrase "the Bible says." They could only get out their Bible, read it out loud, and then make their point.

Likewise, appealing to the "experts" or "scholars" or "science" fails to recognize that experts, scholars, and science almost never reach total consensus about anything. Sloppiness in this realm is unsustainable. I can't count the number of times I have heard someone say in a conversation that "science says" this or that, as though it is some kind of ideological trump card. Science doesn't say a single thing. Different scientists, on the other hand, say many things.

3. We All Apply Experts Subjectively

The way of wisdom certainly includes an honest self-assessment around *why* we draw on the experts. Do we listen to experts because we desire truth, goodness, and virtue, or because we secretly desire to win a war? During one election cycle, immersed in a heated debate with a family member over a particular candidate, I and the family member would come to our exchanges with predictable sources, texts, and podcasts we'd been listening to recently. We lobbed quotes and anecdotes at each other as though they were grenades. I had to repent. What started as two beloved family members dialoguing turned into two combatants, armed to the teeth with a rhetorical army of experts and authorities. Such ideological sparring has become a common feature of late-modern existence, largely exchanging what should be relationships of love with proxy wars for the ideological spirits of the age.

We all are prone to using the hard-earned work of an expert to validate what we already believe. Rather than hearing their witness, we employ them when and if they can fight our battles for us. Dallas Willard argued that this was one of the prices we pay as a society for no longer teaching the basic premises of logic in our higher education institutions. We are given the freedom to learn anything without a mind trained in *how* to use that knowledge. "As a result," Willard wrote, "our world is full of uneducated people with higher degrees. They have no independent logical judgments and simply conform to what their circle takes to be the 'best professional opinion.'"[24] Without critical thinking skills, learning descends into a free-for-all, post-truth society in which, as postmodern philosopher Richard Rorty alleged, truth becomes whatever your contemporaries will let you get away with. Truth becomes nothing more than a "collective hunch."[25]

Take a pause when you find yourself using the hard-earned work of an expert to simply back up what you already think. This is the way of postmodernism—where might is right. With the loss of critical thinking skills, combined with a lost sense of objective truth outside of ourselves, what is true has become an amalgam of our feelings, our community, and our desires.

Many conservatives love scientists when they show us that the being in the womb is indeed a real, living human being. But they hate the same scientists when they tell us that humans are undeniably destroying the environment. And many progressives love scientists when they advocate for health practices that saved lives during a global pandemic. But they hate the same scientists when they affirm that there are, indeed, unquestionable differences between biological males and females.

Our arrogance unmasks our problem. We love winning more than the truth. The Christian listens to *all* the evidence—not just the convenient or politically beneficial parts. And they are even willing to listen to the voice of the dissenting expert who goes against the grain of popular consensus.

4. Expert Knowledge Is Important but Preliminary

Expert knowledge can inform and enrich our lives. But we must recognize that expert knowledge is not the final word on anything. Consider, for example, that just a few decades ago, the medical community declared that smoking cigarettes not only was cool but also had medical benefits. Indeed, in the 1960s and 1970s, industry leaders in medicine were publishing advertisements about the medical benefits of smoking cigarettes. Yes, "expert fallibility" is a reality. We should not forget history. If the experts can and have been wrong in the past, there is a strong chance they will be wrong in the future. "No expert has perfect knowledge," writes Bonnie Kristian. "Some failure is inevitable, and revision after learning is a good thing. It demonstrates trustworthiness, not unreliability, because expert knowledge should increase over time, and experts should change their advice as that happens."[26]

It would not be an appropriate response to believe that experts cannot be trusted at all. If we're going to hold experts to this standard, but not the church for its errors in the Crusades and the Inquisitions and for its widespread silence during World War II, then we are hypocrites. The church has been wrong and has had to learn. So it is with experts. Experts make mistakes, yes! Experts can be wrong, yes! But this does not mean they should be ignored or that they have nothing to teach us.

Theologically speaking, we must remember that the doctrine of sin tells us that all humans "fall short of the glory of God" (Romans 3:23). And so have all their endeavors. To believe that human depravity would not impact expertise does not take seriously our own doctrine of sin.[27] The word *temporary* is embedded within *contemporary*. Contemporary knowledge is what we know now. But give it some time, and it will likely need some revision.

5. An Expert Offers Niche Knowledge

An expert is uniquely qualified to speak with authority about one specific area or domain. When I undertook my doctoral research at the University of Birmingham in the UK, I gave four years of my life to writing the first exhaustive theology of creation care through the lens of a Pentecostal theology of the Holy Spirit.[28] This became the first-ever full-scale doctoral research project on the topic. Since then, many have undertaken my work and built on it to nuance, challenge, and strengthen what I did. But for what it is worth, I was (and perhaps *am*) the world's leading scholar on the topic of Pentecostal eco-pneumatology—a topic that about six people in the world find interesting.

My knowledge is extraordinarily niche, as is the knowledge

of most experts. And experts aren't exempt from the Dunning-Kruger effect in areas outside their expertise. Just because someone has expertise in one area does not mean they have it in *all* areas. No doubt, having such niche knowledge is important. But my expertise in a rather small area of academic theology does not translate into cellular biology, astrophysics, or even into other areas of theology such as predestination or the doctrine of angels. When someone lays out upward of one hundred thousand dollars, devotes four years of their life, spends countless hours reading and writing, and defends their work before a doctoral supervisory board, it should count for something. But authority in one area doesn't translate to authority in every area.

The Expert of All Things

Everyone must risk trusting in someone. But who? When we lose faith in one way of thinking, religion, or ideology, we have not stopped trusting; our trust simply shifts elsewhere. For example, those who do not go to church are more likely to believe in ghosts. And self-reporting as nonreligious greatly increases the likelihood one believes in extraterrestrials and UFOs.[29] Nobody doesn't believe; people just believe *differently*. Even the most secular societies simmer in a lingering religiosity under the surface. In the ever-wise words of the theologian Gerd Theissen, "'Superstition' is a belief rejected in society, and 'religion,' to put it ironically, the officially recognized superstition."[30] Every society is superstitious. The question is simply which superstition is mainstream.

This is why going to a doctor—or any expert for that matter—can be an extension of one's trust in God, especially if their expert knowledge is seen as a gift from God himself. One does not lack faith in God by going to the doctor; one lacks faith in God by failing to see God's healing hand at work through the doctor. This lesson was given to us by King Asa of Judah, who is said to have been "afflicted with a disease in his feet." Asa's sin? "He did not seek help from the LORD, but *only* from the physicians" (2 Chronicles 16:12, italics mine). Stories like this get spun to mean that going to the doctor is the mark of distrust in God. But the problem for Asa wasn't trust in physicians; it was unbelief in God. He failed to see the hand of God at work in the physicians.

How can we trust in God through the knowledge of the expert?

First, be on the lookout for experts who hold the truth rightly. In his second letter, Peter mentions Paul's writings, admitting that his letters "contain some things that are hard to understand, which ignorant and unstable people distort, as they do the other Scriptures, to their own destruction" (2 Peter 3:16). Apparently, having Paul's inspired letters was not enough. Some, it turns out, were misusing, twisting, and manipulating them. Because of this, Paul wrote, "Do your best to present yourself to God as one approved, a worker who does not need to be ashamed and who *correctly handles* the word of truth" (2 Timothy 2:15, italics mine). Having truth is one thing; handling it rightly is another. An expert worth listening to holds their knowledge wisely, humbly, and open to correction.

Second, lend your ears to the humble expert. As the psalmist writes, "Blessed is one who trusts in the LORD, who does not look to the proud, to those who turn aside to false gods" (Psalm 40:4). Here, the godly are forbidden to look toward the proud. How can we heed this? One simple means of distinguishing the humble from the arrogant expert is by paying close attention to how they hold their knowledge. Do they assert grandiose, oversized claims that far outreach their area of expertise? Or do they seek truth at all costs by consistently asking new and humble questions with an openness to being corrected? If so, they have cultivated what has been called "humble inquiry."[31]

Humble inquiry invites self-criticism and seeks to hear criticism offered by others. Humble experts acknowledge how they have been wrong. Their thoughts aren't finished. Nor is their hunger. In theological terms, the expert worth listening to understands their own sinful depravity.[32] It is the prideful spirit that always sees itself as right and everyone else as wrong. But the humble spirit keenly knows its own fallibility.

Third, be cautious of experts who weaponize knowledge for power. In her article "Can We Resurrect Expertise?" Bonnie Kristian points to the portrayal of the experts of the law in the New Testament:

> "Everything they do is done for people to see: They make their phylacteries wide and the tassels on their garments long; they love the place of honor at banquets and the most important seats in the synagogues; they love to be greeted with respect in the marketplaces and to be called 'Rabbi' by others." (Matthew 23:5–7)

Pride is the dark side of expertise. "Experts can have hubris, too," she continues. "With expertise comes the prideful temptation."[33] Indeed, a gift used to coerce is no longer a gift. And too often—even in the days of Jesus—the gifts of expertise to serve God's law were misused for fame, prestige, and power. In a partisan culture like our own, one can see similar power plays right and left. One should almost assuredly be suspicious of any expert who follows a truth claim with "because this is the most important election in history."

Fourth, and finally, we must acknowledge God as the ultimate expert of all things. Paul tells us in Ephesians 1:22 that Christ is head over all things. Not most things. *All.* A Christian assumes that God is the expert of all things. In the words of Dallas Willard, "Jesus is, in fact, the smartest man in my field. He is the smartest man in your field. It doesn't matter what you're doing. If you are running a bank or a mercantile company or a manufacturing plant or a government office or whatever it is, He is the smartest man on the job."[34]

Of any human who ever walked this earth, Jesus is the wisest and most perceptive, knowledgeable, and insightful. This gives us space to hear competing expert claims from fellow humans. When addressing complex issues, we can hear all sides, knowing that God holds the ultimate truth. In doing so, we may end up learning something along the way about Paul's maxim: "Let God be true, and every human being a liar" (Romans 3:4).

Three

Learning from Strangers

Strangers feel stranger than they used to. The collective impact of our diversified, globalized, and decentralized culture has radically altered the way we engage with strangers in the shared civic space. As our society becomes dizzyingly more diverse and tribalized along racial, cultural, and religious lines, there's an increasing sense that we share little to nothing in common with those around us.

We share less and less with each other. Trust and social connection can only happen when something is shared between two people—a language, experience, desire, residence, or religion. All intimacy requires shared experience. But these kinds of shared realities have become few and far between as culture becomes more fragmented. With a diminishing overlap of shared life, there remains an equally diminishing range of topics one can connect over with strangers.

A recent layover at a major American airport offered an epiphany. As has come to be a normal part of airline travel, the flight I was scheduled to be on was significantly delayed. A group of anxious strangers was now sequestered, collectively tapping their toes for the awaited departure. We all got comfortable at the gate. Over a period of ten minutes, three strangers leaned in to talk with me. About what? Each of my new stranger friends was frustrated—as I was—at how bad the airlines had become. Their plight was understandable. This was our shared experience.

The one pressing thing a group of contemporary travelers had in common was frustration with the airline industry. That experience is an instructive parable about our historical moment. We share increasingly little with the strangers around us, yet we still long for connection. So we bond through gripes about how everything runs late, is too expensive, or is underwhelming. Without any shared religion, culture, ethnicity, or history, the lowest common denominator of our shared civic experience is grievance.

Without a shared structure of truth or a universal agreement on the point of life, grievance provides an awkward path toward unity. As former president of the University of California Clark Kerr stated, little more holds together the modern university of today than "a series of individual faculty entrepreneurs held together by a common grievance over parking."[1] Without shared truth, complaint is all that remains. Gripes become the glue of society.

As we are often confronted with people who have diverse ideological, cultural, and religious beliefs, guarding against a deep engagement with the stranger is almost a form of survival. The late urban theorist Jane Jacobs argued that this is a major problem of twentieth- and twenty-first-century cities. When we are constantly surrounded by strangers, she contended, we tend to make strangers out of everyone.[2] As a result, we retreat into neighborhoods of people with the same color of skin, same income, and same general outlook on life.

Pay attention to yourself as you stand in line, cross the street at a crosswalk, or sit on a bus or train surrounded by strangers. The combination of our busyness and our fragmented environment has planted within us what Erving Goffman calls "civil inattention."[3] We look down. We stare at our phones. We insert the earbuds. Why? Because we fear the obligation eye contact threatens to bring. Pay attention to your eyes as you drive to an intersection where an unhoused person asks for help. We've been trained to ignore, look elsewhere, be on our phones. Part of our aversion is to avoid feeling obligated to do something about the plight we see. If we can trick ourselves into believing we don't see—and deceive others into thinking the same—then we protect ourselves against the shame of our inaction and guard ourselves against our guilt for causing pain to someone else made in the imago Dei.

This fragmentation does great damage to our ability to share life with strangers. Sociologists and historians tell us that part of this is connected to how individualistic Western culture has become. In many traditional cultures, the stranger is welcomed and embraced. Finnish philosopher Edward Westermarck wrote a groundbreaking volume in 1906 titled *The Origin and Development of the Moral Ideas.* He explored how traditional cultures could almost universally be identified by radical generosity and hospitality toward the stranger: "The stranger is often welcomed with special marks of honour. The best seat is assigned to him; the best food at the host's disposal is set before him; he takes precedence over all the members of the household; he enjoys extraordinary privileges."[4] In premodern traditional cultures, strangers were not left out in the cold and treated as outsiders. They were welcomed in at all costs.

Our moment looks very different. Look at what we tell children: "Don't talk to strangers"; "Don't take candy from strangers"; "Don't get into a stranger's car." No doubt, it's wise to have a healthy skepticism of strangers. They *can* be dangerous and *may* desire to do us harm. As a child of the 1980s, I vividly recall pictures of missing children on the back of milk cartons outlining details of what the abducted last wore and where they were last seen. The milk industry stopped doing this, but the lasting psychological impact of seeing that kids my age were being kidnapped as I lifted a trembling spoon of Cap'n Crunch to my mouth forged a lasting impression. Even breakfast felt dangerous. In *The Necessity of Strangers*, Alan Gregerman gives voice to this psychological skepticism toward the stranger: "We live in a world filled with strangers and also in a world where most of us have been conditioned to fear or at least avoid people we don't know or understand. People whom we see as different from us in any number of ways and who can seem, by our own quick assessment, to pose a threat."[5]

Those linked memories of milk and kidnapping shaped a whole generation. This has led to the "stranger danger" psychology that is shaping many parents today. But is this fear founded? Sometimes. But sometimes it is not. Unfortunately, we allow the noxious weed of fear to grow out of the soil of just a few painful stories. In his fascinating book *Close to Shore*, Michael Capuzzo writes about the events that took place in the summer of 1916 when a series of shark attacks took place off the shore of New Jersey.[6] The fear that gripped the community led to widespread panic and a mass killing of sharks. Eventually, those events led to the making of the movie *Jaws*. Truth be told, sharks are gentle creatures that rarely attack humans—they are quite scared of them. But a few news reports and Hollywood productions inspired by those events have led to a rampant fear that sharks are out to kill us. We do this to sharks. And we have done it to strangers.

What the movie *Jaws* did to our collective understanding of sharks, stranger danger has done to our culture's perspective on those we don't know. We hear the news of a person pushed onto a subway track by a stranger or a stranger murdering a random person, and we begin to develop an ingrained disdain and fear of strangers. These kinds of experiences are what lead us to construct what philosopher Peter Singer calls "moral circles." We all create a circle of who is in and who is out. In these moral circles, we determine who our people are and who our strangers are. Everyone on the inside is treated well, and everyone on the outside becomes dead to us.[7]

I'm reminded of Alan Gregerman's daughter Carly's response when he told her not to talk with strangers at the bus stop: "But Papa, if I don't talk to strangers, how will I ever make new friends? And how will I ever learn new things?"[8]

Wisdom, Proximity, and Serendipity

There are, naturally, some cautions to name. Is it wise to assume that every stranger is a kidnapper? Absolutely not. Should we believe everything a stranger says? Not even close. We need to be cautious. But the concerning thing is that we have swung to the opposite extreme from the "stranger danger" of my childhood. My generation was taught not to talk to strangers. But now youth are given a smartphone at (on average) twelve or thirteen years old.[9] The stranger now lives in our pockets. We used to tell kids not to take candy from strangers. Now we invite our kids to take most of their ideas from them. And we are all learning that believing the ideas of the stranger can be wildly harmful to developing minds. By trusting the wrong strangers, we see our most vulnerable loved ones being hurt.[10] There's a difference between safe strangers and unsafe strangers. Wisdom is needed to discern which is which.

Even if we don't realize it, we are constantly learning from strangers. Whenever we read a book or newspaper, listen to a podcast, or watch a documentary, we are intentionally taking time to learn from people we don't personally know. We have no problem learning from strangers. Our problem, rather, is that we struggle to learn from strangers who are right in front of us. Which is a rather new historical arrangement. The premodern person spent their life learning from those in front of them, living largely unaware of those who were not. The late-modern person spends their life learning from those they are not with while ignoring the ones standing beside them.

I see this in myself. I attentively learn from the many well-curated, thoughtful individuals who have helped me think deeply about my faith, the Bible, theology, and the state of the world, most of whom I do not know. But I feel weirdly uncomfortable taking the time and energy to learn from the person sitting next to me on a plane, waiting at a crosswalk, or attending a social event. No wonder we're so lonely.

There are ways to reverse this, beginning with a changed perspective. We eventually got on that late flight that everyone was frustrated about. As we taxied from the gate and I stared at my phone, an older gentleman beside me inquired about my destination. Hesitant—and distracted by the onslaught of emails I felt required my attention—I gave curt answers to signal my own disinterest. He soon asked me what I did for a living. I told him I was a theologian. He laughed, looked out the window, and whispered, "What are the odds?" Sensing I should lean in, I asked him what *he* did for a living. "I'm a biblical scholar," he said, "going to a conference." Before long, our conversation was headlong into our research. Turns out, he was one of the leading scholars on funerary practices in the ancient Near East. He told me about one of his academic articles, which I furiously read after I returned home. The research of this stranger entirely changed the way I teach what Jesus meant when he said, "Let the dead bury their own dead" (Luke 9:60).[11]

This serendipitous conversation with a stranger transformed me. What if *every* conversation with a stranger could become a classroom? This is the rationale for seeking to intentionally read books with different perspectives and dialogue with people who are different from us. All of us have blind spots—whether cultural, ideological, or theological—resulting from our own upbringing. This is why listening to the voices of those from different cultures or ethnicities can be so richly rewarding. These experiences can expose our assumptions and biases, which doesn't always happen when we're surrounded by people who look the same as we do. Submitting our thoughts to the scrutinizing story of someone entirely different from us naturally exposes our blind spots. If one of the goals of the Christian life is to walk in truth, these kinds of opportunities can help us become mature people who see the world in as clear a light as possible.

This encounter with a stranger provided an opportunity for what I call accidental learning. This has been called by others "serendipity."[12] What is serendipity? In the internet age, we can scour the internet for the information we are looking for. And—voila—it is there. This kind of learning creates an entirely different problem. In years past, to find information about anything, we had to wade through books and conversations and libraries to find answers. Along the journey, we would learn about things we weren't even looking for. This is serendipity. Serendipity is the learning we never were looking for but got as a prize for the journey. Searchable content shields us from this kind of learning because in a search engine world, we only find what we're looking for.[13] "Where is the wisdom we have lost in knowledge?" T. S. Eliot asked. "Where is the knowledge we have lost in information?"[14].

Strangers pop the bubble. We don't get from strangers what we want or what we are looking for. And that is a gift. Every stranger we interact with may have some accidental knowledge we can carry with us through our lives. There is a long list of stories of how some of the world's greatest inventions came as the result of an individual learning serendipitously from a stranger—such as when Patsy Sherman was trying to create a fluorochemical polymer that could resist deterioration from airliner fuel. The turning point came only after her assistant accidentally spilled some experimental liquid on her shoes that wouldn't come off. The accidental learning eventually led to the invention of a fabric spray that repelled stains.[15] Often, accidents can become our greatest discoveries. Urban myth even holds that the chocolate chip cookie was accidentally invented when Ruth Wakefield spilled chunks of chocolate she was trying to melt for the dough. Thank God these kinds of accidents happen!

Learning from a stranger is possible only if we *desire* to learn. Which, in turn, requires a crucifixion of our own self-satisfaction. When Jesus sent his disciples out into the world to preach, drive out demons, and announce the presence of God's kingdom, he gave them a simple, perplexing command: "Take nothing for the journey except a staff—no bread, no bag, no money in your belts. Wear sandals but not an extra shirt" (Mark 6:8–9).

What is behind this command? By sending the disciples into the world without food, money, or provision, Jesus sent them in a condition of great neediness. For the missionary, this is essential. True ministry is never a one-way street. The disciples were not to go into the world only to give. They were sent with needs. Connections with the lost world became possible because the disciples needed help from the very people they were sent to minister to. In the words of Kenneth Bailey, the disciples "were to go in need of the people to whom they went."[16] Jesus understands the human story. Self-sufficiency spells the end of all relationships. The disciple, then, trusts that God will provide for them *through* others.

This simple teaching, I'm convinced, sets up for each of us a profoundly life-giving ethic for our engagement with strangers. Dependency creates relationships, conversations, and a need for one another. David Smith writes, "To be Christian is, furthermore, not to reserve for oneself the role of host, the one who sets the table, but to learn to see Christ in others, to receive correction from them, to be joined to them, to learn from the stranger."[17]

When the follower of Christ engages with and receives from the stranger, the table is set for a mutually transformative experience. There remain countless volumes in publication on how one can turn a stranger into an asset or new customer in the realms of business, career, or influence.[18] But the idea of a *mutual* engagement with a stranger—where we shape each other—is far less popular. Should we only engage with strangers to get something out of them? Or do we see a relationship with a stranger in a mutually transforming way?

Again, this doesn't mean that everything a stranger offers is good or should be received or believed. Indeed, the serpent came as a stranger in Genesis 3. Not every stranger should be listened to. Without boundaries, we set ourselves up to be greatly harmed. Part of loving a stranger well is knowing where we begin and where we end. To love a stranger doesn't mean losing oneself.[19] God not only creates; God also separates. In saying this, we must recognize the difference between being teachable and being impressionable. The former is the wise posture of learning what to receive and what to reject from the stranger, while the latter is a naive receptivity to everything we encounter.

In the end, though, learning to learn from strangers benefits our Christian formation by positioning us as servants to those in front of us. When we take this posture—as servants who come to wash feet rather than win arguments—we are freed from the compulsive need to "win" every conversation. It is the art of sitting down with someone we do not know and swapping stories, hearing from each other, and sharing space without feeling the need to one-up the other or merely waiting for the other person to finish speaking so we can get our own words in. The gift of the stranger is that they release us from having to walk away as the winner with the best story, anecdote, or quip. The lesson of not needing to compete with our knowledge is hard to learn, but it bears much fruit when we master it.

It is only through practicing intellectual empathy and hospitality that we can enter another person's story.[20] And maybe, Lord willing, share our own.

From Myths to People

We've explored why we should engage strangers. But equally important is *how* we engage strangers. It's a task that often begins with how we think. I love the 1968 short story by celebrated Latin

American novelist Gabriel García Márquez titled *El ahogado más hermoso del mundo* (known to English readers as *The Handsomest Drowned Man in the World*). It tells the mythical tale of a beautiful giant man who mysteriously drowns, washing up on the shore of a quaint village. Surprised and shocked, the villagers find themselves at a loss. Alarmed as they are, they remain strangely drawn to the handsome stranger, whom they call Esteban. After burying him, they continue adorning his grave with flowers and honor befitting a king. The villagers create elaborate stories about who the stranger was, where he might have come from, and why he washed up on their village shore. These myths inspire the village for generations. Márquez's tale invites the reader to imagine how strangers (even *dead* strangers) have the power to transform an entire village.[21]

The power of Márquez's story is that it reminds us that we are prone to create myths about strangers in our minds. The more mysterious someone becomes in our minds, the more we fabricate tales about them. Intimacy has the power to demolish these kinds of myths. With family and friends, we share both proximity and intimacy. Given these familiarities, we are less prone to make myths about those nearest to us. When I lecture through the New Testament, I like pointing out that those who were most intimately connected to Jesus on a family level (his mother, Mary; his brothers, James and Jude; and his cousin, John the Baptist) are each depicted as having worshiped him as the Messiah and Son of God. Historically, this matters. I'd never worship my stepbrother. Nobody would.

Unlike our friends and family, with strangers we have proximity without intimacy. Strangers are near, but they're unknown. No wonder they stir up fears within us. Who is this person next to me on the bus? The possibilities are endless. This stranger could be a world-transforming leader, a famous writer, a future spouse. Or they may run a crime family or be a serial murderer. Who knows? Engaging the stranger could lead to something *very* good or something *very* bad. Indeed, learning from a stranger always incurs risk—to say nothing of loving them.

And so, like Márquez's villagers, we allow our imaginations to run wild around strangers. We catch sight of someone's embroidered red cap touting the return of America's greatness, and we assume we know what kind of person they must be. We bump into someone wearing a rainbow button and believe we know their full story. We observe someone laughing while on their phone as they walk down the street with a pep in their step, and we assume everyone else's life is happy and fulfilled. We see a well-dressed person and are reminded that everyone else seems to fit in, while we clearly don't.

We don't know the stranger—where they're from or how they ended up on the shores of our lives—and so we project our own feelings or attitudes on them. In so doing, we keep them at arm's length. Rather than entering their stories, we fail to appreciate the glory of strangers and their histories, relationships, and experiences. We see in them what we want and who we are.[22] They expose the strangeness of our own hearts.

Recent sociological studies back up this phenomenon. When we find ourselves cut off by a stranger in our car, we're more likely to assume they are the kind of person who voted for the other candidate, thinks differently about sexuality and gender, and holds different religious commitments than we do. Yet when *we* cut off someone else, we blame it on the fact that we're late to soccer practice with our three kids in the back seat. We assume others' mistakes are based on internal factors, but our own come from external factors. We give ourselves grace, but not the stranger. Psychologists call this the "fundamental attribution error."[23] Because we don't know strangers, we assign motives to them. "We think we can easily see into the hearts of others based on the flimsiest of clues," reflects Malcolm Gladwell. "We jump at the chance to judge strangers."[24] This is a well-worn path. But it is not the Jesus path.

The New Testament invites us to think differently about strangers. In Luke 24, two disciples head toward the town of Emmaus after Jesus' resurrection. On the Sunday of the resurrection, they flee in terror: *Are we followers of Jesus going to receive the same punishment Jesus did?* They were apparently unaware that Jesus had risen from the dead that morning. Walking the roughly seven-mile journey from Jerusalem to Emmaus, they happen upon an unsuspecting stranger who strikes up a conversation with them. "What are you discussing together as you walk along?" the stranger asks (v. 17). One of them, Cleopas, responds, "Are you the only one visiting Jerusalem who does not know the things that have happened there in these days?" (v. 18). The stranger retorts, "What things?" (v. 19). They tell him the story of Jesus, ending with how he had died the previous Friday and that "some of our women amazed us" (v. 22) with news of his resurrection.

What myths had they been constructing in their minds about this stranger? Did he just want their money? Or some food? Would he think these disciples were out of their minds? Was this stranger a secret authority sent to detain them? Was he going to report them to the Roman authorities who had killed Jesus?

Arriving in Emmaus, the stranger wants to continue on, but the disciples invite him to stay with them for the night. The stranger obliges. He then does what only the host should do in such a social situation. He "took bread, gave thanks, broke it and began to give it to them" (v. 30). Then, supernaturally, the two disciples *saw*. Their eyes were opened, and they knew who this stranger was—Jesus. They hadn't been talking to a stranger at all; they were eating with the Messiah.

The transformative power of the Emmaus story should have a lasting psychological impact on how followers of Jesus think about strangers. If Jesus came to his followers in the form of a stranger, shouldn't we treat *everyone* as though they may be Jesus? Potent beliefs like these can reverse anyone's entrenched disdain for strangers. Italian philosopher and historian Umberto Eco once pointed out that Marco Polo went to the distant, unknown world because he believed in the existence of unicorns and wanted to find them. And he did! But they were not pink horses with rainbow tails. Polo found the rhinoceros.[25]

Beliefs—true or misplaced—propel action. And by seeing Christ in the stranger, we are compelled to love every stranger. "Do not forget to show hospitality to strangers," the author of Hebrews commands, "for by so doing some people have shown hospitality to angels without knowing it" (Hebrews 13:2). If even God could be disguised as a stranger, so could an angel.[26] To welcome and listen to the stranger could open the door to heavenly messengers sent to serve us.

God and angels, Scripture teaches, come to us in the form of the unfamiliar, the unknown, and even the stranger. Thus, with divine wisdom, it becomes necessary to treat every stranger like an angel—just in case. "We don't show hospitality to be like Jesus," writes Richard Beck. "We show hospitality to *welcome* Jesus."[27] Indeed, to make room for the stranger to be transformed by them is to make room for someone who has been handcrafted by God and imbued with his very image!

To learn from our neighbors—even strangers—we first must obliterate the false ways we have seen them, written them off, and even lied about them. God commands us to "not give false testimony against your neighbor" (Exodus 20:16). This must apply to the way we think about strangers as well. Giving false testimony—believing and enabling lies—against the stranger in either word or thought keeps us from loving them the way God desires. In the novel *Dakota*, Kathleen Norris tells of a catechumen in a Russian Orthodox church. One of the older monks says to a younger one, "I have finally learned to accept people as they are. Whatever they are in the world, a prostitute, a prime minister, it is all the same to me. But sometimes I see a stranger coming up the road and I say, 'Oh, Jesus Christ, is it you again?'"[28]

Perhaps strangers aren't enemies; perhaps they are epiphanies of grace.

Stranger Things in Scripture

Scripture offers us a countercultural imagination toward the stranger—theologically and practically. Antiquity was a scary time for strangers, when they were often ignored or treated as enemies. But things were different among God's people of Israel. In his book *Justice for All*, Jeremiah Unterman describes how dismissive ancient Canaanite religions were toward strangers. Old Testament literature, in contrast, developed an unheard-of ethic of care for the outsider, foreigner, and stranger.[29] For what has been dubbed the "quartet of the vulnerable" (widows, orphans, strangers, and foreigners), there would have been no better place to live than among the people who worshiped Yahweh.[30] So we should not be surprised to see Jesus pick up this perspective in the parable of the sheep and goats in Matthew 25:31–46, where judgment is based on one's care (or lack of care) for the stranger.

Not only did strangers deserve love, but they had much to teach the Israelites as well. For instance, Job—the ancient sufferer—is never explicitly described as an Israelite. He's simply a man from the East (Job 1:3). Scripture doesn't obsess over ensuring that one learns only from the insider.[31] Furthermore, Genesis 20 declares that Abraham has the promise of God reaffirmed by him *through* a pagan king named Abimelek.

Strangers were even provided a Sabbath alongside God's people in Exodus 20:8–11. They were afforded access to Israel's justice system; crops were to be left for the stranger in need; and the meat from an animal that died accidentally was to be given to the stranger at the city gate. This is summed up by the command in Exodus 22:21: "Do not mistreat or oppress a foreigner [Hebrew, *ger*], for you were foreigners [Hebrew, *ger*] in Egypt." This instruction is embodied in the practice of Passover today, where room is to be given to strangers and outsiders to come and enjoy the story of God's redemption of Israel.

With this breathtaking theology came practical guidelines for how one was to interact with strangers. Three core practices shaped the way God's people were to engage in relationship with the stranger: being with, greeting, and talking with strangers.

First, learning from a stranger must entail being with a stranger. In Hebrews 13, the reader is told twice to "not forget." We are told to "not forget to show hospitality to strangers" (v. 2) and to "not forget to do good and to share with others" (v. 16). No other "not forgets" exist in Hebrews. Yet, ironically, we often forget these "forget nots"! To not forget means to not ignore, sidestep, or neglect the stranger. It is for this very reason that the good Samaritan in Luke 10:25–37 is exalted in the teaching ministry of Jesus. When so many people, time and again, had walked past the man in need, there was one who refused to walk on the other side of the road. A Christian ethic around the stranger upholds a commitment to seeing the stranger as worthy of one's energy, time, and attention.

One of the inherent dangers in our modern living arrangements is that we tend to reside in neighborhoods that reflect ourselves. Whether living in the suburbs or the inner city, we are likely cloistered in a neighborhood that (generally) reflects who we are. Bill Donahue, in *The Irresistible Community*, identified the drives for shared experience and shared values as among the things that shape all our social interactions:

> We have an innate desire to fit in and feel good about ourselves as we do life in the company of others. The good news is that a virtually unlimited supply of places are at our disposal—from sports clubs to church groups, from neighborhood bars to local business associations. While some expressions of belonging stray far from the norm, they nonetheless function as examples of our craving for community. Examples include the Pork Belly Ventures bicycle club in Iowa, Star Trek conventions, Lord of the Rings fan clubs, and the American Cheese Society.[32]

The drive to bond through shared interests and clubs is reflected in many of the modern environments we live in. We share life with those who share our interests. And we live in spaces that reflect who and where we are in life. When we are surrounded by only that which reflects ourselves, we can lose touch with those who do not share our ideas, values, or cultural perspectives. Over time, we can become so used to homogeneity that we fail to develop the skills necessary to love those unlike ourselves. Because of this, we find ourselves in fewer and fewer places where we encounter people who are truly different from us.

Second, we must learn to greet the stranger. Being near the stranger makes it possible to encounter them. But proximity isn't enough. A simple "good morning" or a nod and eye contact is a step in the right direction. We show hospitality and do good to a stranger by giving them the gift of our attention. Hospitality does not consist of merely making a meal or hosting someone in our home. It is something we extend to people by offering our attention. As David Smith and Barbara Carvill write, hospitality means "that the stranger not only will be greeted, but also will be given loving attention. The stranger not only will be fed and given a drink; his or her voice also will be granted space. His discomfort will be met with concern, her stories will be heard and responded to."[33]

Greeting a stranger makes the possibility of mutual transformation a reality. Again, modern life has done much to limit our practice of greetings. From banks to supermarkets to restaurants, interactions are mitigated through digital screens and self-checkouts. In his book *The Fall of Public Man*, sociologist Richard Sennett answers the question, What is a city? For him, a city is simply "a human settlement in which strangers are likely to meet."[34] The problem today, he points out, is that the modern world is becoming increasingly automated and digital. In years past, trying to find a park, make it to a restaurant on time, or get the car filled up with gas would require us to interact with a stranger. No longer. The "friction" of living in a city would include the deep need for strangers. Modern cities no longer require humans who need humans. They have become what he calls "individualizing machines" that are "friction-free."[35] Who needs strangers when you have a phone?

In *The Power of Strangers*, Joe Keohane laments that we are losing "those little inefficiencies that force you to interact with strangers—like asking a butcher for grilling tips, or asking for directions, or just ordering pizza over the phone."[36] We are creating environments devoid of greetings.

The command to greet the stranger is structured into Jesus' teaching. "If you greet only your own people, what are you doing more than others?" Jesus asks. "Do not even pagans do that?" (Matthew 5:47). Greetings mattered to Jesus. If our greetings are reserved only for our friends and our family and not for strangers, then something of the Spirit is absent in us. Anyone can love a friend. But there is little that shows the depth of our transformation more than our love for the one we do not know.

Third, and finally, we must talk to strangers. We are given numerous instances of Jesus interacting with people outside his social sphere. In many cases, he intentionally places himself in such a way that a conversation is inevitable. For instance, in John 4, a Samaritan woman comes at noon to a well to retrieve some water. John records, "Jacob's well was there, and Jesus, tired as he was from the journey, sat down by the well" (John 4:6). Most translations of the text seem to show that Jesus is sitting near or around the well that the woman has come to drink from.

New Testament scholar Kenneth Bailey has a fascinating take on this. The text does not say Jesus came to sit "near" the well but "on" the well. Many of the Arabic and Syriac translations make this point clear. Given that wells did not have buckets in the ancient world and the woman has brought her own, Jesus was making a point. "By deliberately sitting on the well without a bucket, Jesus placed himself strategically to be in need of whomever with necessary equipment."[37] In short, Jesus was creating social friction for whatever stranger would come to the well.

Jesus put himself between the woman and what she was looking for to engage in a conversation with a stranger about the nature of eternal life and worship. Modern life is all about getting out of the way to avoid these kinds of conversations. As a professor, I see this every fall and spring. When I was a young man, there were no iPhones to bring to class. So we were left to do something many today would consider insane: We would talk to the strangers in a classroom. Some of us even married these onetime strangers. Students in this new world have a device in their pocket that helps them avoid feeling the need for relationship—and sadly, they use that device as a clever way to hide from their deep longing and hunger for intimacy with others during their college years.

From Strangers to Family

The stranger helps us see the world in a way that would be impossible for us to see on our own. The world becomes more dynamic and electric when we view it through the eyes of another. Thomas Ogletree, former dean of Yale University, wrote powerfully about this:

> To offer hospitality to a stranger is to welcome something new, unfamiliar, and unknown into our life-world. . . . Strangers have stories to tell which we have never heard before, stories which can redirect our seeing and stimulate our imaginations. The stories invite us to view the world from a novel perspective. . . . The stranger does not simply challenge or subvert our assumed world of meaning; she may enrich, even transform, that world.[38]

We do not always choose to encounter strangers. But we must always choose *if* we will learn from them. In 2020, two stories changed everything I believed about strangers. In March of that year, our family invited a Hispanic pastor and his family to live with us as they looked for a new home. Since they were new pastors in a Spanish-speaking congregation in our city, we were told they needed a little support in getting established in a new city. We also looked forward to a much-needed opportunity for cross-cultural engagement. We spoke very little Spanish. And they (except for one of the sons) knew almost no English. They arrived on a rainy spring evening for what we thought would be two or three weeks. Little did we know that the COVID-19 virus would close the world down that very week. For nearly two months, we lived with strangers. The experience of being locked in a home with strangers was, at first, terrifying. But it changed everyone.

That same year, my wife discovered she had an older brother she had never known about following a 23andMe genetic test by her sister. After receiving the surprising news that a stranger shared a genetic match with her—a brother, no less—Steven was welcomed to become a beloved part of our family. From a stranger to family overnight.

That year was the year of the stranger. And I have learned so much from both experiences. From our newfound family member, a whole new dimension of understanding about my wife's family of origin has come to the surface—information that has helped put together pieces of so much of her childhood. And from our newfound friends from Mexico, we learned so much about Mexican culture, heritage, and food. Life in the kitchen will never be the same, to say nothing of making new friends we never would have made otherwise.

Perhaps John Calvin was right when he spoke of the *sensus divinitatis*—an "awareness of divinity"[39]—that is in every person

God has made. Every stranger is an epiphany. And as we begin to come closer to our Creator, we soon come closer to those the Creator has made. The stranger doesn't have to stay strange. Through love, the gospel, and the healing power of the Holy Spirit, the stranger can become (with a little grace) family.

Four

Learning from the Dead

We hate the dead.

In the last one hundred years or so, a revolution has quietly transpired among us. Through a variety of technological and cultural advancements, Western society has slowly convinced itself that the reality of death can be evaded—and those who are dead as well. In *The Denial of Death*, anthropologist Ernest Becker offered a once-in-a-generation exposé exploring the ways this culture—particularly the secular culture of our day—thinks about (or rather, doesn't think about) death. Winner of the Pulitzer Prize in 1974, Becker's work peered into the void of how ineffective the late-modern outlook was in dealing with the crisis of human mortality.[1] Secularism, Becker argued, lacks the resources necessary to provide meaning and transcendence and therefore cope with the darker experiences of human life—death and suffering. So instead we deny these experiences.

The denial of death is the disease of modernism. But historically speaking, our attempts at sidestepping death and the dead are recent privileges. For most of human history, the living dwelled near the dead. Urban theorist Lewis Mumford famously argued that the first human cities were built so people could be close to their beloved dead.[2] Until the beginning of the twentieth century, many human dwellings included a "parlor" in which the body of a beloved would lie for two or three days before burial. My mother shared stories with me of Grandpa Frank, who feared basements because of the dead who often resided down there when he was a child.

Throughout most of history, life and death existed much closer to each other. Now we usher away the dead. I've sat with many people in their final earthly moments, and it has always struck me how quickly the local mortician arrives to usher the deceased from the grieving family to their refrigerated mortuary chambers. We rarely sit with the dead. Instead, we dispose of their remains as quickly as scheduling allows. Charles Reid Jr. cites a *New York Times* op-ed writer who described what Reid called "a new phenomenon in American attitudes about the dead" as "cremation not as an alternative to burial but as an alternative to bother—a way of avoiding 'all that fuss.'"[3] And when bodies are buried, they are embalmed with toxic fluids, sadly making the last act of many a poisoning of the earth.[4]

Even our language seems to deny death. We don't often have "funerals" anymore; we have "celebrations of life." Nobody "dies"; they just "pass." Or they're "late."

But things have not always been like this. Historically, Christians have traditionally sought to honor and revere their dead. When I travel through the UK, I'm shocked how many Anglican churches are surrounded by the dead—literally. Approaching these three-centuries-old church buildings, one often has to meander through sprawling rows of gravestones set atop saints from that church who long ago departed to go the way of God. Churches there are cemeteries. And cemeteries are churches.

In many of these post-Christian European cities, more dead people are buried *around* the church than there are living people *in* the church. And this isn't unique to England. From the eleventh century on, church law mandated that a church was a community that included not merely the building or the worshipers inside, but also the dead who lay around the building.[5] These church landscapes reminded worshipers that the communion of the saints was a communion of both the living and the dead. It dawned on me as I worshiped in one of these British churches that I was literally "surrounded by such a great cloud of witnesses" (Hebrews 12:1). The faith of the dead outside provides the proper shape and structure for the worship of God by the living inside.

This reverence for the dead has longstanding history. Early Christian history reminds us that Christians in the ancient world gathered for worship and the Lord's Supper in the dark chambers of underground catacombs. Not only did these hidden burial sites provide a safe place for Christian celebration to go undetected by Roman authorities, but these catacomb liturgies reminded Christians that they were worshiping God *alongside* the dead. Fourth-century bishop Augustine taught that a Christian burial wasn't for the dead, but rather for the living.[6] Celebrating the dead and being with them was a reminder to the living not to forget their own mortality.

Something is lost when we forget our soon-coming death— namely, the pressing need to turn to the living God today. For thousands of years, church worship was an invitation to return to one's roots, one's family, one's history, and the dead who gave us life. Even a Sunday worship gathering was a *memento mori*—a "reminder of death."

What if, in contrast to our contemporary denial of death, we need the dead? What if we have something to *learn* from them?

Catholic priest and activist Daniel Barrigan spent the end of his ministry and luminous academic career working with people who were dying. Nearing the end of his own life, Barrigan was invited to give a talk at Notre Dame Cathedral. Introduced by one of the nuns, the theologian approached the podium and delivered a short two-minute sermon. His message was simple. He told the audience that it was not the dead who needed him; rather, it was *he* who needed the dead. The dead, as one of Barrigan's colleagues described, were what "grounded him."[7]

Without the dead, we lose our grounding.

Confronting Presentism

Dallas Willard has defined the worldview of Western society over the last century as that which "comes to stand for the rejection of the past as a guide to the present."[8] Progress has become understood as leaving history behind. Indeed, when we decide to learn from the dead, we confront these deep, hidden biases—the worldview of "presentism." Presentism is any belief structure that assumes that the living at any given moment—by having the privilege of still existing—are more virtuous, true, and progressive than those at any other moment in history.

Theologian Bradley Holt defines presentism as "judging all previous ages as inferior to our own."[9] It is, as I tell my students, the presumption that one is right because they exist right *now*. By extension, theological presentism is a belief that one's present knowledge, worldview, and beliefs about God stand in a privileged position over and against those from the past. This outlook has gone by many names—immanentism, historical supremacy, chronocentrism, recency bias, or, as C. S. Lewis humorously called it, "chronological snobbery."[10]

Presentism is everywhere. Look at the internet. Take a moment to search anything. Literally anything. What do you notice about the results? Even the algorithms powering these search engines are created to provide for the searcher the most *recent* and *updated* information on a given topic. This recency bias is built on the presumption that new information is likely the truest and most important information one could need. Even our technology is prejudiced against old information.

Look at our conversations. In a recent disagreement with someone over email, I was told that my children would judge me for my seemingly antiquated perspective on human sexuality. "History will judge you," I was chided. "What will your children and the history books say about you?" As moved as one may be by these rhetorical assaults, some assumptions lie hidden underneath this line of thinking. Apparently, my dialogue partner had insight into the beliefs of future people that I did not. (I wonder if they'll let me borrow their time machine!) And they also held two further assumptions: (1) that the people of the future would be right (never an inevitability, given what we know of human history), and (2) that all people in the future would unquestionably agree with each other. That's to say nothing of the fact that there is virtually no chance I'll make the history books. Comments like these illuminate the presentism alive around us—as well as the hollow and human-centered vision of the future that grounds it.

Presentism is subtle and toxic. It forms arrogant people who believe *their* culture, moment, and outlook will inevitably be proved superior. One could call it intellectual colonialism.

Presentism assumes that the thoughts of today are the gold standard of all time. Scripture disagrees. "The LORD is our judge," the prophet declares (Isaiah 33:22). History does not have a final judgment over us. Nor do our children. Only God's judgment matters. Christian faithfulness comes to expression in our contentment to be on the wrong side of humanity's history books if it means being in God's book of life.

Christians must be willing to learn from history. Why? Because Christianity is a history-affirming religion. We worship the God of history. Scripture testifies that the God of the universe made himself known explicitly by means of historical acts and accounts through real people, moments, and places.[11] It is no coincidence that the incarnation of Jesus Christ follows thirty-nine books of Jewish history (the Old Testament) and an entire chapter of genealogical history (Matthew 1). History is the manger of the gospel.

God stepped into "space and time"[12] to take the form and flesh of a lowly peasant carpenter in a backwater region within the Roman Empire known as Palestine. God entered history. When we forget that we worship the Lord of history, we fabricate a history-less Christianity with a memory that barely extends beyond what happened last week. In forgetting the history that grounds it, Christian spirituality becomes less Christian and more "spiritual," to the detriment of the church's God-given call to form people into Christ's image. Christianity must be historically grounded to remain Christian. Why? Because God has acted in history.

This is why remembering is so important to the God of the Bible. For example, in the Pentateuchal writings of Numbers and Deuteronomy, God constantly commands memory as an operative function of covenant faithfulness (e.g., Numbers

15:37–41; Deuteronomy 5:15). Not only is memory commanded, but remembering *rightly* is core to Israel's worship of Yahweh. For Israel, such divine injunctions were directed at a covenant community that was constantly torn between a desire to retreat to the rich foods of Egypt and a proclivity to entirely forget what God had accomplished in their liberation.

These twin temptations—theological nostalgia (worshiping the past) and theological amnesia (forgetting the past)—consistently got in the way of what God sought to do among his people. To borrow a phrase from sociologist Robert Bellah, Israel was to be a "community of memory" inhabiting and reconstituting the stories of God's faithfulness for future generations.[13] An intimate knowledge of history, as such, was no mere knowledge of facts, timelines, and places. History was inherently formational—the reconstitution of the *lived* faith of those gone before for those who had yet to enter the promised land.[14]

As the Lord of history, God doesn't forget. Nor should his people. A seemingly insignificant line in the middle of Jeremiah's prophetic writings should remind us of this. The prophet records the words of God, who says the bones of the kings will be brought out for all to see. "They will be exposed to the sun and the moon and all the stars of the heavens, which they have loved and served and which they have followed and consulted and worshiped," writes Jeremiah. "They will not be gathered up or buried, but will be like dung lying on the ground" (Jeremiah 8:2). Why does God utter this? God is making a point—an especially important one for a presentist culture. Yahweh is reminding Israel that their history will not and should not be forgotten.

Moreover, history should be their teacher. Jesus reminds us of this: "There is nothing concealed that will not be disclosed, or hidden that will not be made known. What you have said in the dark will be heard in the daylight, and what you have whispered in the ear in the inner rooms will be proclaimed from the roofs" (Luke 12:2–3).

The past has power.

Embracing the Dead

One way to confront the arrogance of presentism is to intentionally practice the discipline of reading the dead as part of our devotion to Christ. Reading the dead can be a discomforting experience for those embedded in a world with an unconscious recency bias. Mark Schwehn, a humanities professor at Valparaiso University, tells a story about assigning the students of one of his courses to read the writings of the fourth-century Christian Augustine. His students didn't understand why they should read him. After all, Augustine was dead, obscure, and out of touch. Schwehn recognizes that he could have better prepared his students to read the dead. Yet he writes of them:

> My students could have overcome my failings had they been sufficiently humble; had they presumed that Augustine's apparent obscurity was *their* problem, not his; and had they presumed that his apparent inconsistencies or excesses were not really the careless errors they took them to be. Humility on this account does not mean uncritical acceptance: it means, in practical terms, the *presumption* of wisdom and authority *in the author*.[15]

Schwehn reminds us that presentism creates a hostility not only toward the dead, but also toward the *ideas* of the dead. Schwehn argues that reading the dead should cultivate humility within the living reader.

Again, this rubs against the grain of our cultural moment. In modern cultures of the West, we tend to believe the present will be judged by the future. (We don't want to be on the wrong side of history!) Through most of human history, though, the present was judged by those in the past.[16] Learning from the dead requires a willingness to sit under the scrutinizing judgment of history as we learn from those we may disagree with. Similarly, losing our connection to the past means we become untethered and unaccountable to anything bigger than ourselves. For the Christian, this is disastrous—and has led to a modern world that was prophetically described by Augusto Del Noce: "Today's man, cut off from the past and from the future, lives through a sequence of discontinuous instants. . . . Perfect novelty is his oxygen."[17]

How can we subvert this? I suggest three main plans of action: reading the dead, reading *about* the dead, and reading *with* the dead.

Reading the Dead

First, we should read the dead—sitting down to hear and receive the words of those who have gone before. This balances our learning and roots our faith in something deeper than the present moment. When we only swim in the thoughts of the living, we place too much pressure on those whose stories have yet to fully resolve. One does not have to think long to come up with a list of fallen Christian celebrities whose flameouts had horrific consequences for people under their care.[18] When the human hero falls, so often does the faith of their followers. We need heroes whose faith and stories have been scrutinized by history—purified by time and critique. In other words, we don't have to wonder if figures from the past will experience an episode of public moral failure; we know the end to their stories.

One of the presenting illnesses of many expressions of contemporary Christian culture is an outlook that cuts the Christian off from history and God's work therein. Too often, we are deceived to believe *our* church, *our* denomination, *our* approach is the best and purest in all of history. Reading the dead buffers us against a form of Christian intellect that goes only as deep as last week's sermon or the history of our own church.

In their book *Surprised by Doubt*, theologians Joshua Chatraw and Jack Carson draw on C. S. Lewis's image of the attic to describe what happens to too many followers of Jesus. Many are deceived, the authors argue, into believing their local church or denomination represents the entirety of the church—and its best expression. This is akin to believing that the attic of a house represents the entire home:

> The problem is that some strands of Christianity do not recognize themselves as simply one room within a larger house. They give the impression that their room (and maybe a select few other rooms) is the entire house. . . . Does this sound all too familiar? If so, you may have long been inhabiting what we call "attic Christianity." If you grew up in the attic of the Christian faith, questioning the walls of your room can feel like questioning the entire house.[19]

But when we grow in our awareness of history and the height and depth and width of the church, we don't have to abandon our faith when our theology or tradition is challenged. In fact, having an awareness of Christian history helps us see that none of our churches and denominations represent the gospel perfectly or purely. We stand in the world together with a church of two thousand years behind us. And this entire church scrutinizes us so we may be sanctified into faithfulness in the present.

The attic is important, but it's only one room in the house. We are part of the church of history, which transcends our own denomination and our local community. Which is why Lewis recommends that Christians read the dead as a discipline. In his introduction to Athanasius's *On the Incarnation*, Lewis offers wise guidance for readers: "It is a good rule, after reading a new book, never to allow yourself another new one till you have read an old one in between. If that is too much for you, you should at least read one old one to every three new ones."[20]

Lewis doesn't believe we should *only* read old books by dead people. "Since I myself am a writer," Lewis endearingly confessed, "I do not wish the ordinary reader to read no modern books."[21] But he does advise balance. As a general rule, growing Christians should consider reading a few books each year by someone who sought to follow Jesus at a time and in a culture entirely different from their own—thereby submitting ourselves to those who have no interest in saying what we want them to say. The dead can bless us through offense.

Reading About the Dead

In addition to reading the dead, it is also instructive to read *about* the dead. Reading biographies can be a revitalizing discipline. A disciple needs someone to follow, not just a set of cold facts. This need drove Paul to invite the church in Corinth to "imitate me" (1 Corinthians 4:16) and "follow my example, as I follow the example of Christ" (1 Corinthians 11:1). These admonitions—broadly categorized under the rubric of the *imitatio Christi*, or the "imitation of Christ"—reveal that just as the disciples followed the person of Jesus, followers of Jesus still need a person to follow in the post-ascension church.[22]

Paul placed parameters around the call to imitate him by correcting the Corinthians for dividing the early church into factions under the names of Paul, Apollos, and Cephas (1 Corinthians 1:12). Yet he corrects others for saying, "I follow Christ," as though they, unlike the rest of the community, don't need earthly human models and accountability. For Paul, following Christ means following some*body*. All Christian formation, even in its earliest iterations, is akin to being an apprentice. As Thomas à Kempis eloquently outlined in *The Imitation of Christ*, being a Christian is learning how to imitate somebody who followed Jesus before you did.[23]

Reading about the dead offers us wise ways to follow Jesus. But it also gives us opportunities to learn from their mistakes. I call these "anti-lessons"—those cautionary tales of the wrong roads our heroes took. We learn from their successes. Why shouldn't we also learn from their mistakes? A gift of biographies is that they allow us to learn from others' mistakes. Most, if not all, teaching hospitals have built this practice into their teaching philosophy. In postmortems, doctors give presentations to each other on the mistakes they made and what can be gained out of them. No doctor is perfect. But every doctor can (and must) learn from their mistakes. Even death has the power to teach.[24]

Consider reading just one biography each year of a saint gone before us. To do so could provide profound spiritual insight for you on your journey with Christ.

Reading with the Dead

Third, and finally, we need to learn to read *with* the dead. Every other year, I teach one of my most cherished courses—a semester-long class titled "Theological Problems." The course takes the student through some of the more difficult theological questions of our time. Previous iterations have covered topics such as sexuality and gender, the Holy Spirit, eschatology, and other seemingly ephemeral topics such as a biblical theology of aliens and Bigfoot that my students find endlessly consequential.

I *love* this class. I require my students to read at least one book by a Christian author who lived before the tenth century. The students often seem confused. Why would a course on contemporary theological problems require a book by someone who lived a thousand years ago? As we go through the syllabus, I unpack my rationale: The best theologians serve the heart of the living by putting our heads together with the dead.

One vexing challenge many of my students bring to the class-room is that they are, as am I, Protestant. Those who come to my class having been formed in Protestant and evangelical cultures often arrive with a deep understanding of the gospel and even the biblical text, but they rarely know much of Christian history. They know the gospel message and the Gospels, but not so much the history of those who passed the good news down to us. Paul House describes this as "theological amnesia."[25] What these students assume to be contemporary crises (such as sexuality and gender, the Holy Spirit, eschatology, and, yes, aliens and Bigfoot) are neither "contemporary" nor "crises." When one knows their history, they are comforted to find that there is nothing new about the challenges Christians face today. The church will not go down in cataclysmic flames because of them. The gates of hell, Jesus taught, have not brought down the church.[26] Nor will anybody's questions.

This is why I require my students to read the dead. As a teacher, I want my students to have a new appreciation for the attic they grew up in and the enormity of the house they never knew existed. What feels like a contemporary crisis is but one of a series of events in the church's two-millennia history that have tested and challenged her. Being a Christian means we see the world *with* the dead. When we do, no crisis is new. And we do not need a new theology to solve these crises. The church's task is never to reinvent theology or make it better. Rather, the task is to retrieve the glorious teachings the church already has in her treasure chest for today's challenges. When we read with the dead, we discover that the church has a word for new theology—*heresy*.

The church is a global, multiethnic, transcultural community that transcends history. This places us squarely within the most diverse community the world has ever seen. This should shape everything about the way we view the world. Years ago, the linguist Stanley Fish wrote a book titled *Is There a Text in This Class?*[27] Part of Fish's project—which was undeniably swayed by some lamentable postmodern assumptions—was to help his readers understand that all people look at the world through the lens of some community. Fish's book provided a renewed appreciation for how "interpretive communities" shape the way people view their world.

Although Fish never directly connected his thesis to the church, following Jesus puts us into the interpretive community of the church that transcends time, space, and culture to faithfully return to Scripture and rightly follow the way of Jesus in each generation. And as we do, God's Spirit will illuminate afresh those stories, images, and themes in Scripture that have been neglected by previous generations. Like Josiah in the Old Testament, the church is called to return time and again to the forgotten Scriptures that lie in the temple space (2 Kings 22).

Every generation must do this. We are never tasked with creating truth; our task is to retrieve it.

Reading with the dead entirely revolutionizes how we understand the Christian faith, think about God, and read the Bible. One of the great traditions of the Protestant Reformation is a belief that every person has the power and privilege to read the sacred Scriptures themselves. This is a profound gift, but it can also be a heavy burden. Many Christians who dedicate themselves to reading the Bible often feel the pressure to perfectly interpret or make sense of what they read. But when we understand that we read the Bible *with* the dead—alongside the church—we come to the text alongside thousands of years of readers, thinkers, and followers of Jesus. Everyone must read the Bible for themselves, but not *by* themselves. We have the privilege of coming to the words of God alongside God's people who have been wrestling with them for generations. This work must be undertaken *together*, in community, among God's people. And it is only as we read the Bible *with* all of God's people throughout history that its power will be manifest.

We could put it this way: This isn't your Bible; this is *our* Bible. Scripture was written by and for communities. And Scripture must be read and interpreted in community. This interpretive community must, for the Christian, include the dead. To read Scripture apart from the whole of the church exposes us to the great danger of making the text mean what we want it to mean. Stanley Hauerwas goes so far as to argue that we should remove Bibles from the pews in churches. His reason? "North American Christians are trained to believe that they are capable of reading the Bible without spiritual or moral transformation."[28] For Hauerwas, we should not be afforded the privilege of reading Scripture by ourselves until we have become the kind of moral and responsible people who have been shaped into Christ's image. Rodney Clapp, too, signals the profound risk of reading the Bible all by ourselves: "To read the Bible apart from community amounts to no less than each reader aspiring to his or her own religion."[29]

We should not take the Bible out of the pews. Nor is reading the Bible by oneself necessarily tantamount to embracing one's own religion. But Hauerwas and Clapp remind us that when we read the Bible by ourselves and for ourselves, apart from the community of people who have been wrestling with it for thousands of years, we greatly heighten the possibility that we will misread it. Thus the importance of reading with the dead.

Nostalgia, Amnesia, and Tradition

Biblical hope is not nostalgic. It arises from a knowledge of the God of the past, present, and future who transcends time and space—the one "who is, and who was, and who is to come" (Revelation 1:8). Does this kind of hope necessitate hiding our heads in the sand of the past? No. Biblical hope is diametrically opposed to nostalgia, which is the worship of the past and an attempt to go back there. Nostalgia says, "We've always done it this way." It harks back to some glitzy, glamorous, seemingly innocent past that was apparently better. Nostalgia tells us to make a nation great again, ignoring that many of those "great" days included enslavement, sexual infidelity, unchecked spousal abuse, women denied the right to vote, and unnamed racisms. Nostalgia says we should embrace the agrarian simplicity of yesteryear and its fidelity to the ground, but rejects the Christian faith that made it possible. In short, nostalgia is being stuck in the past while refusing to worship the God of the present.

Biblical hope is equally opposed to amnesia. Amnesia can come in a passive form of forgetting history and God's actions therein. This is why God is always reminding the Israelites what he has done for them. Throughout the book of Exodus, God consistently frames this or that commandment or statement with the assertion that he is "the LORD who brought you out of Egypt."[30] God's commands only make sense in light of God's provision and grace. To receive God's word, his people must remember what he did to bring them to a place where they might receive it. Too often, however, Israel forgot what God had done.

Amnesia can be passive forgetfulness. But it can also be an active forgetfulness that seeks to "obliterate the past" as an act of power.[31] One of the marks of self-centered human depravity is a desire to control history, to bend it to our ideological liking. Rather than listening to history and what it teaches, we fit it around our desires. This is what Russian Communism did by ravaging the history books of the Eastern countries it subsumed, and why it is still said, "In Russia, it is impossible to predict the past." The authoritarian never receives history; they only seek to remake it to fit their desires.

One of the ways we can walk through these two ditches of nostalgia and amnesia is by developing a healthy relationship with the tradition of the church—reading the stories and anecdotes and biographies of the saints who have gone before us. Christians desperately need the gifts of the dead. These gifts are called "tradition." The word *tradition* comes from the Greek word *tradio*, meaning "to hand down." Christian tradition, then, is the trusted teachings that have been handed down, entrusted to us from the previous generations.

One of the more succinct definitions of tradition comes from Jaroslav Pelikan, who distinguished between tradition and what he called "traditionalism." In his words, "Tradition is the living faith of the dead, traditionalism is the dead faith of the living."[32] Pelikan points out that the toxic use of traditionalism has given tradition a bad image. Being a Christian is one of the most communal, collaborative, and power-sharing enterprises the world has ever seen. When I think about God, I don't get to think alone. I think alongside what John Thompson calls the "allies" of church history.[33]

To talk about such sacred matters puts us in a room with millions of faithful saints who have gained, through their own pain and trial, endless gems of wisdom we can bring to our questions today. None of our questions—and few of our answers—are new. We have at our disposal more glorious insight from two thousand years of history than we ever could have dreamed.

G. K. Chesterton likened tradition to "the democracy of the dead."[34] By this he meant that the Christian is called to follow Christ through the cloud of witnesses who have come before them. For American Christians, this is a jarring thought, for no other reason than our tendency to think of democracy in terms of the collective voice of the living. But Chesterton saw the voice of the church in broader terms. Not only do the living get a voice in what following Jesus entails, but so do the dead. To be a Christian is to submit our lives to those saints who are still with us *and* those who have left us. This is fundamentally different from, say, the Bahá'í faith, which emphasizes the independent search for truth. Truth, for the Christian, isn't the gift of the individual; it is the gift of the entire covenant community of God.

Scripture offers an affirming perspective toward this kind of tradition. Paul, for instance, commands his readers to faithfully receive the gospel that had been handed down to them (1 Corinthians 15:1–4). In the pastoral letters of the New

Testament, there is a strong emphasis on being shown faithful with what has been given (1 Timothy 1:14).

On one hand, tradition was seen as a gift. Over and over, Proverbs invites its reader to receive the well-earned teaching and wisdom of those who have gone before. This kind of accumulated knowledge and insight can have transformative effects. Without it, we experience a gnawing anxiety that we must rethink and reinvent the task of following Jesus in every single generation. Yet at other moments, tradition can be dangerous. For instance, at more than one point, Jesus critiques the dead traditions of the Pharisees and Sadducees as being about "human traditions" rather than the "commands of God" (Mark 7:8; see also Matthew 15:1–6; Mark 7:13). Yet for both Paul and Jesus, their minds were solidly in the pages of the Old Testament.

In the realm of theology, we call this the doctrine of catholicity. The word *catholic* (Greek, *kata holos*) means "according to the whole." The doctrine of catholicity is rooted in the Nicene Creed of the fourth century: "We believe in one, holy, catholic, and apostolic church." The idea here is that Christians do not just believe in their localized expression of the church. They believe in the *whole* church, the global church, the church throughout history that has sought to follow Christ faithfully. To listen to the dead, then, is to collaborate with them on the sacred and ancient way of following Christ.[35] W. H. Auden called this "breaking bread with the dead."[36]

Of course, to embrace tradition—the trusted voices of the dead saints—must come with some cautions in mind. We submit ourselves to the wisdom of tradition by learning and listening and humbling ourselves. But we must not overstep our bounds. In the wisdom of Scripture, the people of Israel were told to honor and respect the dead, but they were never to do what the necromancer does. That is, we are not to speak *to* the dead. In Deuteronomy 18:10–13, God chastises anyone who offers their children in sacrifice, practices divination or sorcery, tells fortunes, or consults the dead. This command put parameters around one's engagement with the dead. We learn from the dead, but we don't worship them. Any form of tradition in which we blithely obey the voice of the dead instead of the Spirit of the living is one God does not honor.

Necromancer Christianity fails to recognize the difference between faithfulness to the living God *through* learning from the dead and faithfulness *to* the dead themselves. Sometimes the dead can be wrong. And any Christianity that fails to understand true worship to God alone ends up replacing the democracy of the dead with a disastrous dictatorship of the dead.

Learning from the dead is like entering into the great potluck of Christian history. Who doesn't love a good potluck? We get to enjoy all the best food everyone has to bring. Having been to a thousand church potlucks, I'm comfortable saying that the worst ones are those where everyone brings either store-bought food or the same thing. Nothing makes a potluck better than everyone bringing their best dishes to the table. The gift of being a Christian is that we have so many important voices to hear and learn from.

Cemetery Learning

Becoming aware of—and interested in—what happened in the past prepares us to be better servants of the kingdom of God in our present moment. Think of it this way. In most university settings, a professor is given some modicum of work called "committee work." Unless they are tenured faculty members, most professors can assume their workload will include facilitating some element of the university's administration. When a committee meeting begins, it is the first task of the committee chair to approve the committee's last meeting's minutes. This ensures two things—that the committee members can agree that what happened *actually* happened and, more important, that each member remembers what already took place in previous meetings.

Occasionally, a new faculty member will join a committee thinking they have all the answers to the questions the committee faces. Yet if they took time to examine the minutes of previous meetings, they would discover that most of their proposed remedies have already been tried. There's nothing worse than a committee member who hasn't read the minutes of the last meeting. They are useless in helping the committee move forward.

Tradition is reading the minutes from the church's previous meeting. To learn from the dead ensures that we have a grasp of what God has already done in the past. And the Bible offers us the resources of the dead so the living can walk wisely into the future.

In a way, this is what makes the seminary experience so potent. I was warned—as are most seminarians—about the dangers of going to seminary. Be very cautious, others would advise, because seminary can become a "cemetery" where our faith goes to die. This well-worn jab is understandable. I know friends who lost their faith in graduate school. The warnings are warranted. But for me, seminary was a different kind of cemetery. It was the place where I was forced to deal with the dead. Perhaps the most transformative aspect of my seminary years was learning to hear from Augustine, Aquinas, Mechthild of Magdeburg, the mystics, Tertullian, Thomas à Kempis, Martin Luther, John Calvin, Karl

Barth, and many more. Up to that point, no one had walked me through the cemetery that had shaped the church that nurtured my love for Jesus.

Jesus expressly desired that we would have our heads in our history books. "Therefore every teacher of the law who has become a disciple in the kingdom of heaven," Jesus taught his disciples, "is like the owner of a house who brings out of his store-room new treasures as well as old" (Matthew 13:52). We need the old treasures for today. The retrieval of Christian history and tradition is itself a confrontation with theological presentism in all its forms. Seminary taught me about ministry in the modern world by forcing me to read the dead. In an information age such as ours, the importance of an environment like a seminary rests not in the fact that it can dispense facts and information. We have the internet for that. If information is the goal, save thousands of dollars and just watch the videos and read the books. Seminary isn't special because it dispenses information.

Seminary is transformative because, as my friend Nijay Gupta puts it, it's a space where Christians can find hope. This is the hope in God's faithfulness that arises time and again from the ashes of our broken, tattered tale of human history.

Seminary changed me. It introduced me to the dead. Without this experience, I fear I'd still be swimming in the shallow end of the present without ever being told that the ocean of the past even existed.

Maybe seminary *is* a cemetery. But that's not a bad thing! In the resurrection of the dead, cemeteries will be very exciting places to be.

Five

Learning from Children

Not long ago, my teaching schedule took me across the country to a seminary in Chicago. I had agreed to give a series of lectures on systematic theology for a cohort of Pentecostal and charismatic pastors and leaders from around the globe. Following what seemed like a successful first day of teaching, a quiet and reserved Hispanic pastor approached me at the conclusion of class. He shared with me that the night before, he'd received a "word from God" in prayer that he believed I was supposed to hear. The message was simple: God wanted me to know that I was a "low-level theologian."

There isn't much that can prepare someone for how to respond to a message like that. In a knee-jerk reaction, I expressed gratitude for my student's boldness in sharing this message with me. He could tell I received the message awkwardly. But I assured him I would reflect on his "word." That evening, I processed in my hotel room what this message might mean for me—and how to respond. My heart oscillated between anger and insecurity. *Who does this guy think he is?* Mostly, I was infuriated. I had to resist the urge to begin class the next day with a "word from God" for him that he was a "low-level student." But something inside invited me to put a pause on my reactivity and ponder what the student had vulnerably shared. As someone who believes God's Spirit can and does speak through people, I was all too familiar with Paul's admonition to meditate on such messages, to "not treat prophecies with contempt but test them all" (1 Thessalonians 5:20–21). I finished the week's lectures and flew home to Eugene. For weeks, the words *low-level theologian* simmered in my soul.

The truth came out. Soon, my curious meditation led to an awareness that God *was* speaking to me through that pastor. God gently confronted a perennial fear I had been harboring in my heart that my life and career were a failure because I hadn't become the accomplished academic theologian many of my peers had. I had always felt a hidden jealousy toward those friends and colleagues who were naturally gifted to excel in academia. But that never came naturally to me. After finishing my PhD, I quickly found that the people I most naturally served were not in the academy. When I tried, I fell flat on my face. In Chicago, God was liberating me to be okay with the truth. He hadn't created me to breathe the rarefied airs of the academic ivory tower. No, my call was to be a theologian who served the people on the ground—the church. I *am* a low-level theologian.[1] God was shattering my shame over my call. That quiet Hispanic pastor had heard from God. The problem wasn't him; it was me.

So much about that experience continues to shape me. I still grieve that I had become the kind of person who would despise being considered lowly. I didn't want to be "low-level." I wanted fame, success, and worldly recognition. I wanted my own ascension. But to do the work God was calling me to, I needed to resist the besetting sin of pride that evermore whispers to each of us that we are better than the place to which God has called us. Blessed are the poor in spirit, the meek, the lowly, Jesus taught his disciples (Matthew 5:3, 5). The way of Jesus is the way of those who are low, small, insignificant, and unseen. What a profoundly offensive thing to say. How can we truly—in a world hell-bent on "making it" and "becoming something"—go against the system and learn to lower ourselves?

In these things, children are our best teachers. Children are a gift from God. More than any others, they show us the virtuous path of lowliness. For many adults, children can prove to be difficult to love, understand, or even be with. This is, in part, because they upend our desired tranquility. They transform us through disruption. We must cut through the claptrap of saying that "they taught me just as much as I taught them" or believing that children see more than adults, as in *The Emperor's New Clothes*. These are shallow clichés—even condescending. These attitudes toward learning from children can feel performative (a kindergarten teacher is expected to acknowledge that they learned from their kids), or children can be granted a mystical power to cut through the facades adults cannot see through. Neither of these approaches require true humility, and they don't paint a realistic picture of children.

The reality is that we are transformed from the inside out by listening to, humbling ourselves before, and learning from the child in our midst. Few would question that adults play a formative—even sustaining—role in the lives of children. Adults provide structure, food, safety, boundaries, baths, touch, physical strength, and moral guidance for the littlest among us. Without the care of an adult, the abandoned child is in great danger. In God's economy, however, adults need children just as much. They provide levity, trust, delight, hope, laughter, and unstructured play that ground adults in real life. We overlook children to our own spiritual detriment. Children have much to teach us. The problem for most adults, again, is their resistance to stoop down, to descend to be with them.

Learning Through Descent

The posture of lowliness and the journey of learning interconnect throughout Scripture. The Bible invites its readers to lower themselves to become teachable people—able to learn from anyone. In the prophetic writings of Job, we find the broken and frustrated sufferer speaking to his friend Zophar:

> "Ask the animals, and they will teach you,
>> or the birds in the sky, and they will tell you;
> or speak to the earth, and it will teach you,
>> or let the fish in the sea inform you.
> Which of all these does not know
>> that the hand of the LORD has done this?"
> (Job 12:7–9)

Job's friends start out well—simply being *with* their suffering friend in the dust of his trauma—but things turn sour the moment they begin offering Job their theological advice. Job's three friends are exemplary . . . until they talk. From that moment forward in Job's narrative, endless religious jargon and bumpersticker theology spew forth. Job learns more from the animals, fish, and the earth beneath his feet than from his friends.

A similar vignette appears in Proverbs 6, where the author instructs the reader to a life of wisdom:

> Go to the ant, you sluggard;
>> consider its ways and be wise!
> It has no commander,
>> no overseer or ruler,
> yet it stores its provisions in summer
>> and gathers its food at harvest. (Proverbs 6:6–8)

Again, notice the invitation. The best teaching is to be received not, as one might assume, in the lecture hall, classroom, or seminar room. No, God's wisdom comes by getting down on one's knees and beholding the lowly ant in its toil.

This same impulse is discernible in Isaiah's prophetic vision of the coming Messiah. In this vision, Isaiah describes a world where predators no longer hunt prey. The wolf lies down with the lamb; the leopard shares space with the goat; the lion won't pounce on the yearling. To cap it off, Isaiah says,

> . . . and a little child will lead them. (Isaiah 11:6)

Years later, the gospel writers pick this up, connecting Isaiah's messianic vision to Jesus. Who was this child Isaiah foresaw? Isaiah's premonition was of the incarnation—of the divine descending to humanity's level, coming down to generously listen, hear, and humble himself at the feet of people. Luke recounts the only story from Jesus' time as a teenager recorded in the New Testament. In the story, Jesus' parents discover him—after going missing for three days—among the Jewish teachers of the law. "After three days they found him in the temple courts," Luke records, "sitting among the teachers, *listening* to them and *asking* them questions" (Luke 2:46, italics mine).

God, as a human child, willingly came to be taught by humans.

This is the incarnation. It is God's audacious humility to come to hear from humanity. God came to be a child in our arms. We, on the other hand, see ourselves as temple teachers rather than those who humbly abandon everything to learn from Jesus.

This brings us full circle to Scripture's invitation to become teachable learners who willingly lower ourselves to places we deem uncomfortable and unthinkable. That is to say, we are wildly discomfited by the notion that God wants us to learn from people and things we believe we are better than. The process of learning goes hand in hand with the journey of humility.

How does God cultivate this kind of lowliness within us?

Adults typically don't enjoy being put in the position of needing to learn from someone younger, less experienced, and less mature than themselves. Consider the teacher's experience. What's to be done when an inquisitive student points out an error in a teacher's presentation or knowledge? When the one in power embraces such correction, a good teacher is made even better. "Instruct the wise and they will be wiser still," the writer of Proverbs tells us (9:9). But too often, the teacher's desire to save face or guard power lures them to double down on their error. In so doing, they are deceived to believe the ancient lie that appearing smart is preferable to truth, or worse, that they are being robbed of their hard-earned authority. But these fears deceive us, and they must be confronted. The best teachers must love the truth more than their power or appearance, even at the price of their pride. A good teacher teaches not only good knowledge; a good teacher teaches *how* to be teachable.

No doubt, this kind of virtue had been percolating in the life of the apostle Peter by the time he wrote his two epistles. He had followed Jesus in person for three years—eventually betraying him just before his crucifixion. Still, Peter had been present at some (if not all) of the most important historical moments in the life of Jesus of Nazareth. He had firsthand experience of Jesus. Yet, in his ensuing writings, Peter was willing to reference and honor the writings of a newer and younger Christian by the name of Paul, who, just years previous, had been seeking to zealously demolish the early Christian movement through persecution. Paul's radical conversion to Jesus on the road to Damascus in Acts 9 changed everything. Peter's willingness to revere God's work in Paul's life—a far less experienced Christian who had not physically walked with or known Jesus—speaks to a life transformation marked by profound humility.[2]

There will come a time in the lives of all those who follow Jesus when they will find themselves being led or pastored by someone younger than them. Nothing gets to our humility (or lack thereof) more than this. If we are attentive, we can envision this as a gift. The truth is, it requires little character to be taught by someone superior to us. But it requires an undeniable amount of character to learn from someone we perceive as inferior. Nothing speaks to the spiritual depth of an adult quite like their ability to sit humbly and receptively under the spiritual leadership of someone younger than themselves—even when their sermons aren't as polished. Learning from those "lower" than ourselves is undeniably painful. But this is how God does his work of forging lowliness. The lowly make us lowly.

A Child Will Lead Them

A primary way God teaches us this kind of humility is through children. If we're honest, this can very well be one of the most painful pathways toward learning for adults. As parents can attest, children often know us the best. They know our virtues, and they know our vices. As Scot McKnight and Laura Barringer write in their reflections on toxic churches, "Kids are natural truth-tellers. We have much to learn from the natural truth-telling tendencies of young children."[3] This is not to say that children do not lie or have the capacity to be deceptive. They are broken humans just as much as any human being. We do not serve children by idealizing them. But they do bear a unique capacity to say the thing others may be unwilling to say. Don't ask the coworker, boss, or neighbor about a father's or mother's character; ask their child. Why? Because children can often be the prophets of a community.

History witnesses to the vital role that children have played as teachers. Think of Anne Sullivan quietly attending to the subtle hand gestures of the child Helen Keller. Sullivan's patience to learn from the blind and deaf Keller eventually resulted in breakthrough upon breakthrough that came to help countless hard-of-hearing and blind people in our own time.

Despite my own misgivings about Sigmund Freud—and I've got many—the German psychologist became one of the first to risk believing that children and their stories were worthy of rigorous academic examination. Freud saw the dreams of children as something worth learning from, a rarity among the nineteenth-century psychological vanguard. Among other things, Freud popularized the notion that children could teach the psychologist something profound about reality and the human condition.[4]

Even the fourth-century bishop Augustine studied the lives and experiences of children to understand human nature. Much of Augustine's written theology reveals a discernible interest in the lives of the young ones around him in his fourth-century moment.[5]

Early on, Albert Einstein learned to harness the brilliance of children for his own scholarship. As his biographers point out, Einstein regularly helped an eight-year-old girl named Adelaide Delong with her homework. On one occasion, Adelaide brought her math questions to the scientist's home, a plate of gooey fudge in hand. Einstein responded, "Come in. I'm sure we can solve it." And solve it they did. After the girl's parents chastised their daughter for disturbing the famous scientist, Einstein told them, "That's quite unnecessary. I'm learning just as much from your child as she is learning from me." Einstein would later tell his friend Louis de Broglie that his goal was to make all his theories so simple that "even a child could understand them."[6] If Einstein couldn't explain his eccentric theories to a child, they would be of no use to adults.

Indeed, children have much to teach. Yet, sadly, they can often go unheard in Christian spaces.[7] In Scripture, Paul was brutally honest about the difficult responsibilities that came alongside getting married and having children (see 1 Corinthians 7). And Jesus commanded the parent to love God most—even more than the child (see Luke 14:26). Of course, these teachings were not intended to create a religious environment wherein children would be abandoned or ignored in the name of God. Rather, they were clear teachings intended to create a community where children can be loved best. God is referred to in the Bible as a "father to the fatherless" (Psalm 68:5). God loves and listens to children.

Yet reading Christian history could leave us with the suspicion that children are hindrances to the work of Christian living and ministry. In John Bunyan's famous seventeenth-century portrayal of discipleship, the hero named Christian puts his fingers in his ears so as not to hear his family and children call out as he leaves to go on his way to the Celestial City. Unfortunately, Christians in the real world have often taken this same approach. Fourth-century writer Tertullian, for example, penned two letters to his wife before his death. His direction? Tertullian strongly urged his wife not to remarry after he passed away because he was convinced that having children hindered the proclamation of the gospel and the work of serving the church. We see the same sentiment in the account *The Martyrdom of Perpetua and Felicity*. These mothers are described as having left their entire lives, including their children, in the name of "martyrdom." O. M. Bakke has gathered a full catalog of stories of Christian parents leaving their children in the name of leaving society to enter monastic life that would break anyone's heart.[8]

In the writings of some of the church's mystics, we discover time and again that they, as children, had visions and dreams about Jesus. But they often kept silent because they knew if they dared share these secret revelations, they would be locked up or considered insane.[9] Children who heard from God were often institutionalized or ignored by the church. Furthermore, children are (at best) an oblique topic in modern theological circles. In fact, the first formal, academic biblical/theological writing on the topic wasn't published in print until 1892, when Earl Barnes wrote an academic article in the journal *The Pedagogical Seminary* titled "Theological Life of a California Child."[10] Theology has tended to be the thinking *of* adults *for* adults.

Thankfully, shifts are beginning to take place. In his book *Children and the Theologians*, Jerome Berryman calls attention to the famed *Last Supper* by Leonardo da Vinci. While many of the disciples of Jesus would have had wives and children, Berryman shows us that they are entirely omitted, forgotten, not even considered in the famous painting. Of course, a Passover meal would not have been a meal for the men alone. More likely than not, the wives and children of the disciples would have been present as well. One painter named Bohdan Piasecki decided to right this wrong and completed a repainting of the *Last Supper*. In his 1989 painting, Piasecki included an artistic depiction of the Last Supper with children and wives present. The result, let's just say, is an entirely different portrayal of the night before Jesus' death.[11] And a more historically accurate one.

And while little had been written in the realm of the theology of children before the twentieth century, a renaissance on the topic has been afoot in recent years, not only in theology but also in biblical studies. One biblical scholar, Marcia Bunge, undertook a grant-supported study to explore the role that children play in the story of the Bible. What she found was a storyline replete with children.[12]

Another development is the child theology movement, which has sought to reintegrate the importance of children into the realm of theology. This movement is so convinced that children can and should be included in theological dialogue that it will only do theology as long as children are present.[13] While this may seem extreme—as I suspect many may feel—it nonetheless shows that when children are in the room in which we do theology, we tend to be kinder, humbler, more generous, and more open to play and wonder. As every parent knows, we talk differently when children are around.

The Vulnerability of Children

We must lower ourselves to be taught by children, but we must do so with intention and great care. Life for the child has always been a vulnerable experience. In the ancient world, children played a vital role in agrarian life. Farming and shepherding were impossible without the young, to say nothing of the fact that children were, for all intents and purposes, the social safety net of the family in antiquity. There were no 401(k)s or retirement plans. Instead, families had children. This is why many ancient pagan religions spent so much time and energy seeking the blessing of their many gods so they might be assured of offspring. Pagan fertility cults, as they are called, offered deceptive hopes to navigate the scary intersection of childbearing, subsistence living, and a tumultuous economy. Without children, existence was virtually impossible.

Despite children's importance, the experience of a child in those ancient contexts was terrifying. In the first century, up to half of all children would not survive to their fifth birthday because of illness or unforeseen complications. For this very reason, it was common in many cultures to not even name a child until the first week had passed. Why name someone, it was thought, if they weren't going to live long enough to be known? Things were only made worse by the fact that the Roman Empire legally permitted and encouraged "exposure," an evil practice in which unwanted children (mostly girls and babies with birth defects) were taken outside a city gate and placed in the wilderness to die from the elements or for animals to devour. Rough estimates suggest that one out of three children succumbed to death by means of this grotesque practice.

Social hardships further made life difficult for children. The world looked down on them, seeing them as least in the hierarchy of cultural power structures. We get whiffs of this kind of negativity in the Gospels. Matthew recounts two such instances. In one, Jesus' hometown of Nazareth refused to give a hearing to Jesus' message upon his inaugural return. Matthew says about those in Nazareth that "they took offense at him" (Matthew 13:57). Why? An entire town could not receive him or his kingdom because they had known Jesus as a child. They didn't want that kind of God—one who embraced the lowliness of childhood. On another occasion, a group of unnamed adults bring their children to Jesus. The scowl of the disciples is immediately discernible: "But the disciples rebuked them" (Matthew 19:13). These accounts are underscored by the fact that the Greek word for "child" in the New Testament, *paidi*, has the same root as the word translated "slave woman" or "servant girl." There even appear to be linguistic hints of disdain for children.

Undertones of similar negativity toward children constantly swirl around us in this modern moment. Notice the speed with which we describe our least favorite politician, celebrity, or thought leader as "acting like a child." This seemingly mild critique sees childhood as the lowest common denominator for human stupidity and folly. We compare our least favorite people to children.

Children are vulnerable beings. This is why we must approach them—to learn, listen, and receive—with great care and sensitivity. A friend once described to me what he experienced every time his father preached in the church. As a child, when he would enter the sanctuary where his father had just taught Scripture, my friend could immediately tell from the congregants' looks that his dad had used him as an illustration. Everyone knew something about him that he hadn't given them permission to know. He wanted to be a child, not an illustration. Children shouldn't play such roles without their permission. As the first generation of children whose parents were on social media are entering adulthood, there is a strong pushback against oversharing about one's child on the internet. Many are beginning say that "sharenting" has the power to greatly impact the mental well-being of the child in the present or in the future.[14]

Rather than guarding children as vulnerable beings, we treat them as props for the needs, wants, and ideologies of adults. Adults too often treat children like the daughter of Herodias, who danced for Herod. Herod loved the little girl's dance. He was pleased, and he promised to give the girl whatever she wanted. Her mother—still seething that John the Baptist had denounced her marriage to Herod—instructed her daughter to tell Herod that she wanted the head of John the Baptist (Matthew 14:1–12).

Children often pay the heaviest price for the malformed hearts of the adults in their lives. Psychologist Carl Jung (alongside Sigmund Freud) helped bring attention to ways the inner lives of adults can have a profound impact on the lives of children. "Nothing has a stronger influence psychologically . . . on their children," Jung writes, "than the unlived life of the parent."[15] In other words, children can become oppressed by the unlived hopes, desires, and wants of the adult. Just watch the parents in the stands at a sporting event for their children. We can so easily make our children proxies to help mitigate and manage our own dashed dreams. As public theologian Andy Crouch wisely stated, children tend to pay the heaviest price for the delusions of adults. Speaking about the harm that our digital technologies can have on the littlest among us, he wrote these words:

> On the scale of the history of human religions, Western culture's entire 200-year-old experiment with the gods of technology is at its very beginning. Who is to say that in 500 years those gods will seem as benevolent, or as potent, as

they did in the 20th century? Over and over again through history, with inexorable logic, idols end up demanding the ultimate sacrifice, even while they stop rewarding us. That ultimate sacrifice is, of course, human beings. Especially the most precious and vulnerable human beings: children.[16]

And sadly, this kind of harm done to children through the dangerous thinking of adults is seen around us all the time. Children—embodying the fanciful thinking of the culture in which they are raised—are irreparably cutting their bodies in the name of "finding themselves." The gender revolution has been so quick and seemingly unstoppable that even the eyes of New Testament scholar N. T. Wright have turned toward it. In a rare editorial entry titled "Letter to the Editor on Gnosticism," Wright offers a rare critique of the ideologies of our time by drawing a clear connection between the fanciful gods that adults worship and their impact on children:

Sir, The articles by Clare Foges ("Gender-fluid world is muddling young minds," July 27) and Hugo Rifkind ("Social media is making gender meaningless," Aug 1), and the letters about children wanting to be pandas (July 29), dogs or mermaids (Aug 1), show that the confusion about gender identity is a modern and now internet-fuelled, form of the ancient philosophy of Gnosticism. The Gnostic, one who "knows," has discovered the secret of "who I really am." . . . This involves denying the goodness, or even the ultimate reality, of the natural world. Nature, however, tends to strike back, with the likely victims in this case being vulnerable and impressionable youngsters who, as confused adults, will pay the price for their elders' fashionable fantasies.[17]

Children can easily be overpowered by adults. They know they *have* to listen to us. But adults don't always believe they have to listen to children. What if we did? I tend toward workaholism, as do many in my profession. During an especially busy season, I was faced with a decision about whether to accept a particular invitation. If I said yes, it would take me away from home for one week. If I said no, I'd be giving up a remarkable opportunity to grow in my vocation and calling. I asked a friend for help with this difficult decision, and he gave me a challenging assignment. He told me to ask my five-year-old son what he thought. In doing so, I would be giving my son power, voice, and an opportunity to speak into what would happen. This terrified me. But I did it. My son quivered as I asked, telling me he didn't want me to go. I knew what the right choice was. It was my son or my career, and I needed to listen to my boy.

Historically and down to this very day, children have been among the most vulnerable people in society. Because they are so vulnerable, to listen to them is not just lending them a voice; it is giving up power. It is making ourselves vulnerable too. Children, we must remember, are not props to be utilized. They are not inconveniences to be ignored. They are not insurance policies on which to pin our hopes or avatars through which we can live vicariously. They are image-bearing people who should be protected and who deserve to be heard.

Jesus and the Children

Yet, oddly, the New Testament rarely speaks of children. Only three times, in fact, are the words of children recorded in the Gospels. The first is when Peter sits in the courtyard of the high priest's house, and a servant girl says to him, "This man was with him" (Luke 22:56). The second is the account of Jesus' disappearance for three days in Jerusalem at the age of twelve. The young Jesus asks his parents, "Why were you searching for me? Didn't you know I had to be in my Father's house?" (Luke 2:49). In the third account, Jesus enters the same temple space as an adult to overturn the tables of the money changers. Soon after, the chief priests and teachers of the law are outraged by the children who declare over Jesus, "Hosanna to the Son of David" (Matthew 21:15–16). Jesus then quotes Psalm 8:2 to them: "From the lips of children and infants you, Lord, have called forth your praise."

Ironically, the theologians of Jesus' time couldn't see Jesus for who he was. But the children apparently could. In two of these accounts, children are in the temple space. In one, the words are from the God who came as a child; in the other, the words are of children worshiping God incarnate. When children speak in the New Testament, their words are directly tied to the identity of Jesus as the Son of God.

Jesus' own interactions with children would have caught anyone's eye in the first century. We can see in the way Jesus valued children that he embodied a countercultural perspective toward the littlest in society. Moreover, the way he operated his ministry demanded that his disciples were often in close proximity to children. To be near Jesus was to be near the children. Matthew records one prominent account:

> Then people brought little children to Jesus for him to place his hands on them and pray for them. But the disciples rebuked them.
>
> Jesus said, "Let the little children come to me, and do not

hinder them, for the kingdom of heaven belongs to such as these." When he had placed his hands on them, he went on from there. (Matthew 19:13–15)

This brief account must be read in light of the story that precedes it. In the previous section of Matthew's gospel, Jesus was teaching on divorce and marriage. Jesus addressed the issue of eunuchs, those who had their genitalia rendered useless by birth, coercion, or choice. In other words, a eunuch is one who cannot have children of natural descent.

How might this teaching about eunuchs help us see what is going on with the children coming to Jesus? Note that in the story of the children, people—presumably parents—are bringing their children to Jesus. In the teaching on eunuchs, Jesus is illustrating the kingdom by speaking about people who *cannot* have children. And here, Jesus is illustrating true kingdom living by focusing on children and, by extension, those who *could* have children—in other words, people who recognize that he is a better shepherd than they are and that their children are in safer and better hands than their own.

One wonders if Jesus is dismantling the commonly believed notions that our identity is solely tied to our ability to have children and that the children under our care are "our" children. These two stories invite the reader to think twice about our presumed notions of "adulthood" and to put children and the capacity to have children in the hands of Christ.

In placing children over adults, Jesus is doing something in the formation of adult disciples through these children. In her book *Gender and Grace*, Mary Stewart Van Leeuwen considers how often Jesus centers social relationships (such as parenting) around the kingdom of God:

Jesus does not disparage relationships; he affirms the created sociability of persons, and he uses homey illustrations from family and village life in his parables. He also affirms parenthood as an important calling for both men and women and a role that deserves respect from children. But he does not allow these roles to take precedence over the kingdom of God. He does not allow them to be idolized.[18]

Did you notice that the disciples do not want the children to come to Jesus? Reading this account, we must remember who is present. Jesus is likely around thirty years old at this point. The children being brought to Jesus are likely younger than ten—they are called "little children" by Matthew. But the disciples who are offended that the children have come—how old are they? The interpretive key to this story is the fact that these disciples were not much older than the little children. Most of the disciples were likely teenagers themselves, ranging between thirteen and eighteen years old. The indignation they feel is not the feeling of an older person with a young person. It is anger toward those *just a little younger* than themselves. Jesus is not merely confronting their low view of children; he is confronting a kind of pride that can easily come into the heart of a disciple. And he confronts the pride in our own hearts as God's children who look down on any of God's other children who are just a little lower than we are.

The children with Jesus do not do what the adults around Jesus usually do—we have no record of them asking Jesus a single question. This is not why the children come to Jesus. Adults come to Jesus to get something from him; children in the Gospels come to Jesus to be *with* him. As Jerome Berryman points out, "They are not even interested in what Jesus is saying! What they are interested in is Jesus *himself*."[19] One can only imagine: Would they have simply wanted to play with Jesus? And would Jesus have been one of the few adults they'd encounter who simply wanted to play with them? Adults want to discuss things with Jesus; children simply want to sit on his lap. No wonder the disciples rebuke them. In their minds, the work of the kingdom would have left no time for play. But their agenda was vastly different from the agenda of Jesus.

And it is to these little ones that the kingdom is nearest. God is said in Scripture to hide the secrets of the kingdom from the "wise and learned" and to give them to "little children" (Matthew 11:25). And if he places these secrets with children, wouldn't it make sense that we have to go to children to receive them? Jesus is teaching the disciples—and us—the gift of humility. The way of the child is the way of poverty of spirit.[20] This humility is learned as one spends more and more time with Jesus.[21]

And so when Paul writes his letter to the church at Ephesus and speaks to the "fathers" and the "mothers" in the room about what good and right Christian living looks like, we should not ignore the fact that he *also* addresses children. The earliest Christian communities put the entire family together under the teaching of Jesus. The children were in the room. When Paul writes, "Fathers, do not exasperate your children; instead, bring them up in the training and instruction of the Lord" (Ephesians 6:4), he is doing so with the children sitting right there and watching. In the Christian community, Paul teaches the children through correcting the parents in their midst. Paul knew what he was doing. The humility behind the parents' willingness to repent in the presence of the children teaches the children to humbly follow Jesus for the rest of their lives.

When I choose to learn from a child—my son, a student, someone "below" me—I receive two gifts: (1) I am given the gift of humility, and (2), I am giving the gift of humility. To learn from a child is to model for them what a maturing adult who wants to love God should look like. We shape our children by what we teach them. But we transform them by *how* we learn from them.

As a teacher, I've realized that this is the greatest gift I bring to the classroom. My greatest gift is not what I teach; it is infecting my students with a wonder to want to be taught by God. Which is why my feelings were not hurt when I received what I considered to be the best course evaluation of all time: "I don't know what the class was about, but Dr. Swoboda was really excited about it." My students learn from me as I passionately learn alongside them.

A Child in the Midst

As I mull over the account of how Jesus welcomed children, I find myself drawn to Matthew's phrase that the children were "in the midst of them" (Matthew 18:2 ESV). That one line has a brilliance—a kind of luminescence—that leaps off the page. The children were *there*, in the middle, with Jesus fully present to them. These children were not only brought to Jesus; they were placed, it seems, by Jesus himself among the disciples. As we reflect on this imagery, we can't help but wonder what Jesus is doing at our present moment. Is he, again, trying to place children in our midst?

I believe so. This, I should say, does not make things easier. Quite the opposite, in fact. Children have a way of disrupting the lives of adults. I vividly remember realizing after our son was born that our long, untouched, undisturbed mornings of ecstasy in prayer and Bible reading had come to a screeching halt. Those mornings free and clear to be with Jesus were quickly replaced with feedings, diaper changes, and screaming. My child robbed me of the precious time with God I held so dear. Still, as I matured, I came to receive this disruption as the gift a child brings. With children, spiritual life can no longer be done only on our terms. Children, it turns out, bring us to God in a whole new set of ways we never would have imagined.

By placing children among us, Jesus displaces many of the things adults cherish about their lives. They expose the busyness we love—a busyness rooted in pride. Screens have replaced relationships, games have diminished conversation, and distraction has conquered intimacy. Kids always pay the biggest price. For centuries, the minds of children have been nourished by parents without phones who read them stories.[22] But who has time to read to children anymore? Just hand them an iPhone or iPad. I am complicit. Rather than sit down to talk and eat with my own child, I'm tempted to tinker with apps and check emails.

Technological interference—or what sociologists call technoference—is wreaking havoc on our ability to simply sit and be with a child.[23] There are a variety of ways to see how technology is hindering our relationship with children. "Do to others as you would have them do to you," Jesus taught in Luke 6:31. How are we to believe that children will sit with us when we are old if we were unwilling to sit with them when they were young?

Children also expose our lack of joy, play, and imagination. Children laugh way more than adults. In fact, the average adult laughs a mere four or five times a day. The healthy child, however, will laugh about three hundred times a day.[24] One of the sad signs that we have lost a childlike heart is to no longer smile over meaningless stuff. "After childhood," theologian Ronald Rolheiser writes, "we rarely find it easy to delight in anything."[25] We were meant, like a child, to live with real and robust imaginations. Children bring us into their world—the world of play, of make-believe, of imagination. In fact, adults who had imaginary friends as children are more confident, better adjusted, and less neurotic as adults. They are also better able to let others win at games.[26]

With joy, children arouse good questions and curiosity. Curiosity—the delight of learning new things—is a gift of the Holy Spirit. Theologian John Webster writes:

> It is the mission of the Holy Spirit to realize and preserve this new intellectual nature. The Holy Spirit is the Lord and giver of life; he so works upon and in reconciled creatures that the new nature comes to be their own. Intellectual dispositions that had fallen asleep are awakened at the Spirit's approach; powers that had ebbed away and dissipated are restored and concentrated; desires that had scattered into chaos are directed to what is good and holy. And so the intellect begins once again to move, and by the breath of the Spirit there arises a new intellectual *life* corresponding to the new intellectual nature.[27]

Often it is through children that God awakens this kind of curiosity within an adult. On average, a child asks between three and four hundred questions a day.[28] They bring into our lives the gift of sheer curiosity. They desire to learn, see, experience, even taste, everything. There's no end in sight. This can be hard for us adults. We like our patterns, our set ways, our predictability. But the child holds our hand and leads us into a whole world of curious play, a curiosity that is a gift of the Holy Spirit.

This is the gift of being *with* the child. During the COVID-19 pandemic, our family decided to invest in a hot tub.

We did this for one reason. The pandemic brought up every question in the world for our son, and he needed a place to ask his questions. Nightly, we would sit in that tub and talk out the difficult questions of life. We talked about everything. It was there that we first began the "birds and the bees" talk. That hot tub began our evening routine of conversation. Some of those conversations were the most sacred I've ever experienced.

Children, I learned, ask the most important questions. They ask questions adults would never think to ask. They name reality and expose our ignorance. Sadly, though, as we become older, we stop asking the same number of questions. Maybe this is why C. S. Lewis wrote so many letters to children, which was a hallmark of his literary career.[29] As he became more and more famous, he remained connected to children who read his work. He was never dismissive, never curt, and never spoke down to them. He saw children as full image bearers of the living God. He even drew little pictures in those letters.

Interestingly, Lewis continued to write to children as his wife Joy was dying of cancer. He even ended many of his letters by asking the child to pray for him. Maybe Lewis was onto something. Jesus was interested in loving children, but he was also interested in the formation of his disciples. And he knew what he was doing when he invited children to be in their midst—questions and all. Lewis, like Jesus, understood the power of staying connected to children and learning from them.

Lewis wisely quipped that when God dreams of the kind of people he is making us into, he wants within us "a child's heart, but a grown-up's head."[30]

Six

Learning from Parents

A Christian geneticist once shared with me his fascinating reflections on the genetic makeup of Jesus, given his miraculous conception. Most children are the genetic combination of two people—a biological male and a biological female. This explains the mole on my forehead (which I inherited from Mom) and my beautiful Czech skin (which I got from Dad). I'm a two-in-one being—as are *most* humans. Not Jesus, however. What would Jesus' genetic makeup have looked like, given his virgin birth? My geneticist colleague opined that Jesus wouldn't have looked a smidge like Joseph. Nobody would have said, "Joseph, that kid has your complexion. He looks just like you." Jesus would have been *all* Mary—Mary's chin, Mary's skin color, Mary's eye shape, Mary's posture. That Jesus did not look like Joseph could conceivably have made Mary's life that much harder, given the incredible nature of her story. The sheer absence of Joseph's complexion in her son likely added to the growing suspicion among many that Mary had been lying all along. Before Jesus carried his cross, Mary had her own.

Parents give themselves to their children. They also introduce children to the world. Genetics aside, we must not ignore the impact that Mary and Joseph had on Jesus the human. Jesus would have picked up their mannerisms, their quirks, their idiosyncrasies. He learned how to wash dishes like they did. And he picked up parts of their outlook on the world. We are all transformed by our parents, for better and for worse. If parents got a quarter every time their children uttered the same careless words they heard their parents use, the cost of all future therapy sessions would be covered in spades. Indeed, we reap what we sow.

But this raises a problem. Why, in his divine brilliance, would God bestow such glorious little creations into the hands of such broken caretakers? This keeps most parents up at night. Why would God put me under the care of two people who had as much baggage as my parents did? More to the point, why would he put my son under *my* care? Part of my own growth has been the recognition that I am the broken gift God has for my son. I wish I were not the man I am, and I wish my son could have better than he does. But I do not get to choose these things. "My greatest sin, Lord Christ," Jesuit priest William Breault poetically penned, "is that I don't want to be a sinner!"[1] That's my sin too. In pride, I think God should know better than to give a beloved child to me.

Psychology has long sought to understand the parent-child relationship—as it gives shape to our lives—and how we are impacted by the people who brought us into the world. Psychologist Carl Rogers argued that healthy, well-adjusted people need two essential things to be learners in life—boundaries and acceptance.[2] Children need parents who can establish boundaries that promote safety and clarity. But they also need a space where they can come as they are, loved and nurtured in their present state. Much of the child's adult health, Rogers believed, was intertwined with the security of the parent.

Other psychologists, such as the British psychologist Donald Winnicott, believed that if the emotions of a child were not given full acceptance in their family of origin, their unvoiced emotions would tend to be perverted later in life. His famous example is the child who could not express anger at the feminine authority in his life and turned to degrading sexual violence toward women later in life. When the parent could not create emotional space for the child, Winnicott theorized, emotions would come out in unhealthy ways as an adult.[3]

While I don't have the training to agree or disagree with this vanguard of psychologists, I do know this: We were all given a caretaker—be they biological, adopted, or foster—from whom to learn. Parents are an integral part of God's design for our formation as human beings. While we may call God "Father" as we pray the Lord's Prayer, we must not imagine that God replaces (or *seeks* to replace) our human caretakers or parents. The gravity of our parents' lives pulls at us until the day we die. Sure, God is *like* a parent. "As nurses commonly do with infants," John Calvin wrote in his *Institutes*, "who even of slight intelligence does not understand that . . . God is wont in a measure to 'lisp' in speaking to us?"[4] God loves and nurtures us as a parent should. But God is no replacement for our earthly parents. God never breastfed us, read to us at night, taught us the alphabet, or sat us down for a talk about the birds and the bees. These things were tasks best undertaken by the broken, finite, unsanctified humans we know as our parents.

One thing is inescapable: Everyone will learn from their parents. For many, we will learn from years of love, care, and nurture. When the parent-child relationship is undertaken with sacred care and intention, it will give the child a foundation on which they can leap into the joys of life. This relationship will provide invaluable lessons, wisdom, and insight for a flourishing human life. Others of us will need to learn from the fractured lives of our parents or caretakers. Rather than learning from our parents what we *should* do, we learn what we ought not to do. We may need years of receiving from God his wisdom to know what would be best to unlearn (like that deep sigh I breathe, so familiar to everyone in my family, when I'm disappointed or annoyed). That sigh isn't original to me. So little of who we are is original. I got the sigh from my dad. And he learned it from his dad. Learning is often learning what we want to change. But still, we will all learn from our parents.

"Honor your father and your mother," God instructs us in Exodus 20:12. When we read this commandment, it is interesting to note who it is given to. When we look at the fourth commandment about the Sabbath, which came just before this one, we notice that God says sons and daughters should also be given a day of rest (v. 10). The structure of the command assumes it is being given to the parents of the children so that their little ones would be given rest. So when we read the fifth commandment about honoring our parents, we must upload our knowledge that this command appears to be given primarily to adults. This adds a new dimension to understanding honor. When we were children, we had no choice but to learn from our parents. But as adults, we *choose* to hear, learn from, and honor our parents— not something that comes easily. There is a lurking temptation to believe that once we have moved on from our childhood, we have nothing more to learn from those who brought us into this world.

To "honor"—as the commandment states—means to esteem, value, and offer great respect. But this is only one side of honor. It is one thing to name, appreciate, and receive all the good our parents did in and for us. But the more difficult part of honoring our parents is being willing to name the ways they harmed, wounded, and kept us from becoming the people God created us to become. We must do this for our parents. And we must be ready (Lord have mercy) for our children to do the same for us. Honor is not just a saccharine baptism of everything from one's childhood as though our parents were perfect angels. No, honoring a mother or father is respecting them too much to honor the sin that enslaved their lives. Honor blesses. And at times it confronts. Whatever the case, honor often entails our willingness to learn from and be taught by our parents.

Ghosting

When we are children, we mostly do not have a choice of whether to have a relationship with our parents. But as we grow older, those relationships are no longer compulsory. The adult child gets to *choose* to be in a relationship with the parent. This freedom to relate (or not relate) to the parent is almost entirely the function of developments from the Industrial Revolution of the eighteenth and nineteenth centuries. Among many other things, societal shifts from that period of time led to profound changes in parent-child relationships.

How?

Prior to the Industrial Revolution, the way humans related to land and place was profoundly different. Before the invention of the engine, a person would likely spend their life working on one farm or in one city, or at one particular locale where they lived. The Industrial Revolution drastically altered the way goods and services were produced. It was a revolution in *how* and *where* people spent their time. Soon, it became feasible to live in one place and work in another.

The opportunities that resulted were innumerable. Recreation at faraway locations became possible. Working somewhere far from home was soon a new ideal—even a mark of affluence. These shifts profoundly impacted the way humans related to the places and spaces from which they came. And with this came a radical change in how people related to those who brought them into the world. The young were given the opportunity of moving away from home to discover themselves and make their own life. No question, much of this was beneficial. Still, it led to a new way of existing, where relating to parents was optional rather than required. Many no longer needed to live near their parents after graduating from high school or college.

These technological advances have brought many blessings but also great woundings to the modern person. More than ever, human society has siloed off into fragmented groups of ages and generations that live apart from other ages and generations. Too often, we build our churches on this principle—kids with kids, singles with singles, adults with adults, and the old with the old. We tend, by law of affinity, to gravitate toward those who are like us. Sociologists show us that as we experience vast upgrades in technology, the walls of the age ghettos of American society get thicker and thicker. Unlike in the ancient world, the parent no longer *needs* the child, because they have a 401(k). And the child no longer needs the parent because they have the internet. Sociologist Elisabeth Lasch-Quinn comments on the dramatic impacts of these changes on the parent-child relationship:

> In the nineteenth and twentieth century America, functions once performed by the family were transferred to other

institutions. The media and the school, for instance, have taken up much of the role of educating children. As a result, many parents have lost their intimate, firsthand knowledge of their children—just the kind of knowledge that makes it possible to enjoy the company of children.[5]

Given that we are no longer compelled to remain in long-term relationships with our parents and grandparents, our capacity to navigate differences begins to atrophy. The modern inability to love the different, I submit, is a direct result of a society that opted for freedom over covenant and relationship. The result, in the words of Philip Rieff, is heartbreaking: "Crowded more and more together, we are learning to live more distantly from one another, in strategically varied and numerous contacts, rather than in the oppressive warmth of family and a few friends."[6]

We see this everywhere. At my university, as well as at others, a crisis has been manifesting for years. The story is almost normal now. An incoming freshman moves into the dorms, starting off their new semester with a new roommate. Soon thereafter, as if out of nowhere, said new student simply disappears from the university. In academia, these are called "ghost students." Without warning or explanation, students are simply leaving. What's going on? Administrators usually discover that this sudden departure had little to do with teachers, finances, or even academics. All too often, the student got frustrated with their roommate over something trivial (like cleaning the dishes) and lacked the skills needed to navigate the relational friction.

Increasingly, my students do not have robust intergenerational relationships. As a result, they come with a lot of information but not much wisdom. This reality shapes much of what I do as a teacher. Anyone can download a lecture, I've heard it said, but nobody can download a mentor. This is remarkably true. My students do not come to my classroom anymore—or even to me—for information. They have that in spades. They come to me because they need wisdom for walking in a world of complexity.

The phenomenon of ghosting (or leaving without notice) is not unique to higher education. This is a common experience in late-modern America. Employees leave their jobs without giving notice; boyfriends or girlfriends stop responding to texts; congregants leave without warning at the slightest quibble over last week's sermon. Navigating differences is a lost art. Rather than learning the skills necessary to love those who see things differently than ourselves, many people find it easier just to end the relationship.

Modern life has made this permissible through social mobility, overreliance on electronic communication, and tribalism. We are able to separate ourselves from those we disagree with. The problem of ghosting is not just a crisis for the academy; it is a crisis for humanity. Our mobility and lack of commitment have kept us from developing the skills necessary to form deep, meaningful, and trusted relationships with those who are fundamentally different from us. This is particularly true in how we relate to those who are older than we are, who are from a different generation or who see the world in a very different way. There comes a point in most modern individuals' lives when knowing their parents or grandparents becomes a matter of choice, of privilege, of decision. And severing those relationships can have a devastating impact.

Intergenerational Intelligence

One way to view the breakdown between parents and children is through the study of intelligence. This has been a growing field for decades—not without its land mines. In their book *The Bell Curve*, Richard Herrnstein and Charles Murray looked at the story of intelligence through the lens of genetics. They postulated that there is a direct connection between race/genetics and one's intelligence. In the end, they argued for what they dubbed the "cognitive elite." The best genes, they sought to establish, were isolated from those of the genetic underclass. They wrote, "The irony is that as America equalizes the [environmental] circumstances of people's lives, the remaining differences in intelligence are increasingly determined by differences in genes. . . . Putting it all together, success and failure in the American economy, and all that goes with it, are increasingly a matter of the genes that people inherit."[7]

Rightfully, their ideas were squarely rejected by the broader academic community. But outside of the academy, their work had a massive influence. Selling more than three hundred thousand copies, their text set in motion for many the idea that one's ethnic or racial history or background provided a genetic inheritance that made or broke someone. The subtle racism has been called out by many.

Those in the field of intelligence took issue with the fact that Murray and Herrnstein overlooked the environmental components of one's intelligence. That is, how we learn has more to do with the environment of our upbringing than the blood we received from our ancestors. This spurred a whole new field called "social epigenetics," which seeks to explore the intricate relationship between environment and intelligence. This field was popularized by a 1999 study of London cabdrivers by Eleanor Maguire. What Maguire and her team found was that the part of the brain that connects to spatial recognition—the *posterior hippocampus*—for cabdrivers was found to be significantly larger than that of those who were not cabdrivers.[8] It was discovered that, to some extent, one's environment had the potential to literally change the structure of a person's brain.

This finding carries great weight for how we think about learning from our parents in our family of origin. The very structure of our minds and the way we think are impacted by the relationships in those most formative years. This has given rise to another field called "intergenerational intelligence," which can be understood as the collective and individual constellation of knowledge and wisdom garnered from relationships with people from different generations.

The idea that intelligence and environment are interconnected has been fleshed out in the work of David Shenk. He writes in *The Genius in All of Us* that violinists in the twenty-first century have shown the capacity to grow in their skill much faster than in previous generations. "There is an explanation," he argues. "Some people are training harder—and smarter—than before. We're better at stuff because we've figured out how to *become* better. Talent is not a thing; it's a *process*."[9] Others, such as Shinichi Suzuki—who developed the Suzuki method of learning music— have shown us that children learn music best when they learn in the right nurturing and encouraging environment. In short, we will learn from our parents. And how they teach us matters.

Intergenerational intelligence provides a compelling framework from which to consider human development. This was the setting for my developing a love for baseball, tomatoes, and Halloween—from my mother. It can also help us understand our greatest fears, which are often tied to real events in our lives. Sometimes, though, fears lie under the surface of our consciousness. In a recent study, researchers introduced into a group of male mice the scent of acetophenone, which smells like cherries and almonds. As the scent was introduced, the mice were shocked with electricity so the smell became associated with pain. Naturally, the mice began experiencing anxiety whenever the smell was introduced. When the next generation of mice were introduced to the smell—without the shock—the mice immediately manifested an anxious response. So it was in each subsequent generation. This revealed that fear in the mice was not necessarily connected to a lived experience. Rather, it was passed along intergenerationally from parents to offspring.[10] Humans are different from mice. But it does raise the question: Is your fear of spiders because of an actual spider? Or is it because you saw one or both of your parents be afraid of a spider?

This experiment shows that much of what we learn from our parents is not taught but caught. Consequently, a parent must closely attend not merely to *what* they say to their child but also to *how* they say it. The heartbreaking writings of Christopher Robin Milne, the biological son of A. A. Milne, illustrate this need. Most readers of *Winnie the Pooh* would assume that the writings must have come from the hand of a father in touch with children. But this wasn't the case. Milne was distant, shy, and disengaged toward his son. And his stories conveyed that which he never conveyed in person. His father's distant disposition eventually led Christopher to a break from his father and the church.[11]

We don't just pick up words from our parents; we pick up fears, emotions, and shame too. A child psychologist once warned me never to say the word *ewww* in disgust when a child goes to the bathroom or talks about body parts. This can, over time, inculcate deep levels of bodily shame. Kids pick that stuff up. It can have lifelong consequences. Research has shown that children's brains can recognize and remember the emotional experience of shame even before they acquire the ability to speak.[12]

Intergenerational Friction

One's relationship to a generation older or younger than their own is called intergenerationality. It's a repeated theme in the Bible. We see it occurring in reference to Judah's kings in the phrase "he did evil in the eyes of the LORD, just as his father had done."[13] These children, it seems, picked up the ways of their parents—and not for the best. Similarly, parents are instructed throughout Scripture to teach their children the ways of the Lord. In Deuteronomy 6 and 11, parents are told to teach the ways of the Torah to the children. The call of a parent is to pass along the faith to teach, mold, and shape the child.

This theme of intergenerationality provides the rationale for the whole book of Deuteronomy. When we come to Deuteronomy 5–6, we find that the Israelites have been freed from Egypt, spent a year at Mount Sinai, and wandered for thirty-eight years in the wilderness. Now they are preparing to enter the promised land on the other side of the Jordan River. But there is a problem. After thirty-eight years in the wilderness, there are many people who weren't present at Mount Sinai when the Law was delivered. Many who had been there have died. A whole new generation needs to be taught the Law.

When we read these chapters in Deuteronomy, we notice that the Ten Commandments are repeated from Exodus 20, albeit in a slightly different manner. Seemingly tiny twists reveal that the same old Law is being given to a new generation. E. D. Hirsch Jr. famously called this "acculturation," the process whereby the things of God are handed down to a new generation.[14] The need for acculturation provides the very literary structure for the book of Proverbs. Many of the proverbs are about the passing along of wisdom from father to son. Three times in Proverbs 1 alone—and twenty-four times total in Proverbs—the author explicitly states that wisdom is being given to the younger generation through the older. We hear this in Proverbs 1:

The proverbs of Solomon son of David, king of Israel:

for gaining wisdom and instruction;
    for understanding words of insight;
for receiving instruction in prudent behavior,
    doing what is right and just and fair;
for giving prudence to those who are simple,
    knowledge and discretion to the young—
let the wise listen and add to their learning,
    and let the discerning get guidance—
for understanding proverbs and parables,
    the sayings and riddles of the wise.
(Proverbs 1:1–6)

And finally, in Paul's letter to the church in Ephesus, we read what scholars commonly call a household code. The apostle outlines what an appropriate Christian community should look like in a normal family system. Paul commands the kids, "Children, obey your parents in the Lord, for this is right. 'Honor your father and mother'—which is the first commandment with a promise—'so that it may go well with you and that you may enjoy long life on the earth'" (Ephesians 6:1–3). This reveals (given that it was read out loud) that children were in the early Christian worship gatherings. They were not in some other room with people their own age. Parents and children were learning together about how to engage with each other. Fathers didn't travel to a parenting conference to learn how to love their kids back home. And kids weren't taught how to honor their parents in a kids program while their parents sat in "big church." Learning took place in the same room—together.

These biblical examples bear witness to the generational diversity known among people under God's rule. I call this intergenerational friction. It is the difficult challenge that comes with people of different generations being in close proximity. It doesn't make things easier; it makes things profoundly more difficult. And the result is very formative. In the end, we can be deeply transformed by learning to love people who are fundamentally different from ourselves.

When children and adults are together, intergenerational friction develops depth of character. Many churches today offer two different kinds of services—one for the old people and one for the young people. We call these "traditional" and "contemporary" worship. And there is nothing wrong with this practice. But it often sidesteps the difficulty and blessing that come with two different generations sharing one room. The older individuals in the church get the music turned down in one service, while the younger ones get things amped up in the other. Over time, we are presented the gospel solely in our own generational context rather than having to walk alongside those who are different from ourselves. As a result, we soon create a number of worship domains where everyone hears the biblical account on their own terms and for their own needs and desires.

Intergenerational friction produces patience in the old and the young. Before my grandfather Rudy passed away, I began noticing that his memory was fading. As we went fishing, he would tell me the same stories he had told a hundred times before. The lapses in memory were endearing—sometimes.

But these repetitions became equally frustrating. I had to learn to put up with it the way one learns to put up with watching the same commercial over and over again. Still, this repetitive narrative formed something in me. It built into me deepening patience. I couldn't just abandon him on those long fishing trips in a stinky truck. I had to listen, over and over and over again, to the same old stories. Most of my students are not raised around their grandparents. But when they are, I find that their ability to deal with differences in class is significantly heightened.

The result of diminishing togetherness means we no longer work the conversational muscles necessary for good learning. In a book titled *A Is for Ox*, Barry Sanders surmised that this was one of the dangers of too much television—it means we do not have to practice mutual dialogue. "Speaking sentences to another human being, listening for a response, marshalling thoughts in order to respond again, and on and on, encourages a person to care about other people. . . . In the exchange of stories, the hope arises, as the poet Robert Browning writes, that the other will 'rap and knock and enter in our soul.'"[15]

When I think about my grandfather at that stage in his life, I remember how slow he became. A simple drive to the gas station seemingly took forever. One can only wonder what it would have been like to walk through the wilderness on the way to the promised land for thirty-eight years with the older generation that had been in Egypt, knew the stories of the Red Sea, and had seen Moses come down from Mount Sinai. The past generation slows everything down. And every temptation stirs within us to just leave them in the dust so we can get to our destination faster. As narrated in A. N. Wilson's biography of C. S. Lewis, it was during the most fruitful season of Lewis's life that the needs of his adopted mother occupied much of his attention—from yard work to doing the dishes.[16] Lewis could have written much more had these needs not been so great. But perhaps by slowing down, Lewis became the man we know and admire.

Intergenerational friction deepens our capacity for love. In 2016, during the presidential election, it became evident that my mother and I had profoundly different perspectives on the direction our nation was taking and who should be the president. Up to that point, we had politely managed to sidestep any major arguments or disagreements. Slowly, I began to sense within myself a buildup of internal resentment about why I thought she voted the way she did. And she felt the same way toward me. Our differences soon came to the fore, and we had to be honest with each other.

One night, it almost came to blows. We stayed up until three in the morning arguing, being angry with each other, and even yelling at one point. Then it became clear—we both were doing our best with the information we had. This required that I put down my biases and assumptions—not assigning motive—and hear what she had to say. And she had to do the same. We did not leave that conversation agreeing with each other, but we did leave it *trusting* each other. I learned that she had given deep thought to her decision (even if I disagreed with it). And she extended the same trust to me.

This was a rare moment for my generation. Many parent-child relationships have been severed as a result of not knowing how to navigate these kinds of tensions. My generation—like an odd replay of the Abraham and Lot story—goes to the left when the parent goes to the right, or to the right when the parent goes to the left.

This experience taught me—and continues to teach me—that my mother brings to her perspective of the world a very different set of values, expectations, and hopes than I do. We both are committed to our Christian faith. And we want to see God reign in all things. But our outlooks on the world could not be more different in the realm of politics. For many, these differences can lead to a cold apathy where we opt for silence instead of honesty. Too often, we choose to sidestep truthfulness to avoid confrontation with those who have gone before us. Or worse yet, we let confrontation end a relationship.

Finally, intergenerational friction develops wisdom. Each generation brings unique gifts. The older generation brings wisdom, stories, and hindsight; the younger generation brings knowledge and information about what is and what is not a scam. We need each other. When the generations come together, we have a collective memory—thus Scripture's repeated invocation to remember history. An intimate knowledge of history is no mere collection of facts, timelines, and places. History is inherently formational—the reconstitution of the *lived* faith of those gone before for those who have yet to enter the promised land.[17]

A kind of mutuality is born out of these intergenerational relationships. I saw the benefits of intergenerational relationships in my relationship with my mom when she first started sending texts. I had to teach her how a phone works, what not to do in a text, and the nature of an emoticon. She, on the other hand, gave me a life of wisdom from her own experience. The mutual exchange is powerful. She passes along the wisdom that comes from years of hard-earned errors and folly. And I help her discern from the information she is receiving what is and what is not spam. We have learned the lesson that we desperately need each other to flourish in this world.

Learning as Jesus Learned

It may be true that the older we become, the less information we will learn from our parents. And that is okay. The goal of the Christian life is not to pilfer information from someone so much as it is to live in increasing intimacy and oneness with them. The goal of learning for the Christian is not the absorption of content; rather, it is entering into deeper and more intimate relationships. As time goes on, we may receive less and less from our parents by way of knowledge or insight. But we may increase in intimacy.

We learn this from Jesus.

Jesus Christ is God in the flesh. As a true human being, Jesus had parents. We can feel overwhelmed as we consider the mystery of this reality. The God who created the first parents (Adam and Eve) enters the story of humanity by, quite paradoxically, being *parented*. What a glorious mystery! God takes on an earthly mother and father. But Joseph disappears very early in Jesus' life. When we look at Jesus' relationship with his parents—aside from a few early stories—the absence of Joseph is notable. Somewhere after Jesus' teen years, Joseph is no longer in the picture. What happened?

One clue is given in Mark 6. In the ancient world of Jesus, a son would carry on the family business. Jesus would have spent his childhood apprenticing in his father's business as a carpenter. That is why Jesus is called the "carpenter's son" in the Gospels (Matthew 13:55). He was likely under his father's business—for a time. Something odd transpires in the language of Mark 6 as Jesus is no longer called the son of the carpenter. Suddenly he becomes "the carpenter" (v. 3). Jesus, it appears, is now running the family business. Many New Testament scholars have surmised that this little change in language could signify that

Joseph—Jesus' earthly caretaker—had died and the business had been handed to the son.

Again, consider the mystery of all of this. Jesus—the incarnate Son of God—would have spent his formative years learning from Joseph the ins and outs of running the family's first-century carpentry business. Jesus would have submitted himself to a rigorous regime of learning and growing in this craft. Would Jesus, the true human, have had to learn from his humanity? Would he ever have hit his thumb with a hammer? Would he have cut the wood a little off the desired angle or dropped a rock on his toe? Did Jesus have to actually *learn* from his father? Or did he already know everything and only pretend to learn the trade?

The author of the letter to the Hebrews wrote, "Son though he was, he learned obedience from what he suffered and, once made perfect, he became the source of eternal salvation for all who obey him" (Hebrews 5:8–9).

Jesus learned?

The dangers of trying to make more of this than we should are numerous. But it is worth considering the mystery: Jesus, God incarnate, *learned*. If Jesus was a true human—as Christians have believed for two millennia—then wouldn't he have had to learn how to walk at some point in his life? Would Jesus have had to be potty trained? Someone had to have taught Jesus the alphabet and the daily duties of doing dishes, feeding the animals, and folding laundry—activities Jesus still knew how to do in his resurrection body, right? (Yes, Jesus appears to have folded the laundry in the empty tomb!)

If Jesus is God, and God knows everything, how could Jesus learn? Can someone who knows all things *learn*?

To be truthful, I'm uncomfortable with any answer that suggests that Jesus was incomplete—as though Jesus needed to become an improved human being. I resonate with the thinking of the twentieth-century German theologian Karl Barth, who disbelieved the liberal German theology of his time that saw Jesus as the ideal, evolved, perfected human. Along with Barth, I say *nein* (German for *no*). Jesus is not an idealized and perfected human. This is not the teaching of the incarnation. Jesus did not *become* divine through learning and growth. Barth famously said, "One can not speak of God simply by speaking of man in a loud voice."[18] The story of the incarnation is not Jesus becoming the ideal human; it points to the truth that God descended into our footsteps to rescue us in our sin and brokenness. The incarnation is God entering our story and embracing a full human experience.[19]

The clue to understanding this paradox, I believe, is in the phrase "once made perfect" in Hebrews 5:9. By no means does this mean Jesus was not perfect. Quite the opposite, in fact. Rather, Jesus took on full humanity to reveal his full perfection. By becoming a human, Jesus was revealed as the perfect one. For if the Son did not become a human, humanity could not be helped. One of the leading New Testament scholars on the book of Hebrews, George Guthrie, explains what he sees the author saying here: "Perfection is Jesus going through an experience that he hasn't been through before in order to get to the place where he can meet the need that God had designed him to meet in our lives in new covenant priesthood. The incarnation means that the Son of God experienced things that he had not experienced before."[20]

As a human, Jesus learned. Our problem is that we think learning involves taking in new content or information. This is not the kind of learning Jesus experienced. By learning, Jesus was entering our story, hearing us speak, and entering true intimacy with humanity. God had never been a human before this. God had never been taught how to wash the dishes. God had never lived in a body. In fact, as Jesus returns to glory with the Father, he ascends having experienced something he had never experienced before—humanity.

Jesus *learned* humanity.

And he learned a lot of it from his mother. It is not scandalous that Jesus learned from his parents. Rather, it is scandalous to believe that one can truly love without entering a relationship. When Jesus encountered a man who had been disabled for years and learned about his condition (John 5:6), he wasn't taking in new information. This was the God of the universe. Rather, Jesus was entering in to lovingly hear the man's story.

The older I get, the more I am tempted to believe I have nothing more to learn from my parents. Thank God for the incarnation. Even Jesus—the one who knows it all—committed himself to be one who learned from his parents. If Jesus was willing, how much more should we be willing?

Seven

Learning from Secular Culture

One of the most influential figures in the early church was Jerome (345–420). He had been raised in a privileged Christian family in what is modern-day Slovenia. As a nineteen-year-old, he made a consequential decision to uproot himself and move to Rome, where he'd be afforded an education second to none. At some point during his time in Rome, Jerome was baptized. Soon thereafter, he set out to travel the world. As he experienced exotic cultures and peoples, Jerome fell in love with the literature, artistry, and ideas of the pagans he encountered from distant lands. Then came the dream.

During Lent of 375, Jerome woke up from a vivid and powerful vision in which he had been ushered into the presence of God. During this experience, God—or as Jerome described it, "the voice"—corrected him, saying, *Ciceronianus es, non Christianus.* Roughly translated, this means, "You are a follower of Cicero, not of Christ." Waking from his disturbing encounter, Jerome confessed his guilty conscience. Indeed, he had loved the writings of pagans over the sacred writings of Scripture. Jerome would never be the same, promising a renewed, unflinching commitment to the Scriptures. He soon abandoned the writings of the pagans.[1]

Something of Jerome's youthful zeal can be discerned in many moments throughout the history of the church. As I became a Christian in the 1990s, many young evangelicals were being told to leave behind the music of secular culture. I still remember the day—as if it were yesterday—at a youth conference in Seattle, Washington, when we were told from the stage that our AC/DC, Eurythmics, and Michael Jackson albums ought to be thrown away or burned. Many in my generation followed this advice, including some of my friends who destroyed their entire collection of non-Christian music.

Ironically, the later writings of Jerome reveal that the author eventually returned to the very writings he said he'd never read again. Was this a mistake? Did Jerome backslide from God's command? Or did the wisdom of maturity give him a new perspective on how to engage with the secular culture of his day?

How should Christians engage with the non-Christian culture around them? And does that culture have things we can learn from?

These are not new questions. The earliest Christians faced many pressures, few of which were as pressing as developing a new set of skills to engage with (or disengage with) the cultures in which they were placed. Should Christians continue to be involved in the life of their broader culture? Would it be appropriate, for example, to continue visiting the shows at the Roman Colosseum, with their displays of godless violence and bloodshed? Would their witness to Christ demand their involvement in these major social activities? Or should they pull away from social engagement completely? These questions were highly consequential for the nascent church in the years following Jesus' ascension.

New Testament scholar Michael Gorman captures the weight of these questions for the earliest church:

> These believers were faced with hard questions and decisions. Should they continue to participate in social activities that have a pagan . . . religious character? This would include most activities: watching or participating in athletic and rhetorical contexts; buying and eating meat in the precincts of pagan temples; and frequenting trade guilds, clubs, and events in private homes.[2]

Given the transformative power of the gospel of Jesus that they had been entrusted with, rightly fleshing this out couldn't have been more consequential for the early Christian church. They had a mission given by Jesus to take his message to the whole world. One of the earliest attempts to answer the question of social engagement was made by Tertullian in *The Prescription Against Heretics* (Latin, *De praescriptionibus adversus haereticos*). It reveals just how challenging understanding Christian identity in a hostile Roman world had become. In Tertullian's treatise, two worlds are at odds with each other: Athens and Jerusalem. Athens represented the pagan world of philosophy, science, and worldly knowledge, while Jerusalem represented the world of faith, revelation, and divine knowledge. In it, Tertullian famously asks, "What indeed has Athens to do with Jerusalem?"[3] For him, the church was fundamentally out of sync with the world it was in.

The importance of this conversation isn't isolated to antiquity. The relationship between divine and worldly knowledge continues to simmer beneath many of the conversations in the church today. Consider a case study. When we think about how a church functions—what she does and how she does it—is our task to simply go to the Bible to discover the template? Or is it permissible to learn from the broader culture to gather wisdom for how we "do church"? I recall this debate playing out quite often in my seminary courses. Should a pastor glean wisdom from business leaders for their task? If memory serves me correctly, a fistfight nearly broke out in that seminary classroom.

This issue is further complicated by the fact that Christians respond to questions like these in a myriad of ways. For some, Athens has nothing to offer Jerusalem. They are diametrically opposed to one another. Views like this one can run both ways, with some saying the church shouldn't learn from the world and others that the church has nothing to teach the world. As such, a wall of separation is erected between them. And to be clear, from the Christian perspective, *some* skepticism has its basis in wisdom. "Don't you know that friendship with the world," James warned, "means enmity against God?" (James 4:4).

A healthy outlook should entail a form of Christian skepticism that resists the urge to unthinkingly believe the curriculum of culture simply because it's embraced by many or most people. Just because the majority believe something does not ensure its truthfulness. Discernment is needed—especially in a post-truth culture that bends to the peer pressure of the present. This kind of healthy skepticism was espoused by Christian author Flannery O'Connor in her college years: "What kept me a sceptic in college was precisely my Christian faith. It always said: wait, don't bite on this, get a wider picture, continue to read."[4] O'Connor's words are saturated with wisdom.

Still, wouldn't it be odd for God to excuse himself from the world he made? Indeed, to borrow the words of one theologian,

"It would be strange if the Spirit excused himself from the very arena of culture where people search for meaning."[5] Either Jesus is the Lord of all or the lordship of Jesus only applies to the church. Again, Christian skepticism can be healthy. But we also must learn to embrace the Spirit who can and does speak wherever and through whomever he wills. Former seminary president Richard Mouw tells an insightful story about a businessman who had become a Christian. Mouw describes an academic theologian who was disgusted by the fact that this new Christian described Jesus as his CEO, which the theologian called "tacky." Naturally, the businessman was coming to faith from the context of his own lived experience. About this, Mouw writes:

> Was this tacky theology? Perhaps. But, then, maybe there is something to be said for tackiness. We might even think of many of Jesus' parables as a kind of sanctified tackiness. Jesus borrowed mundane images from ordinary life to talk about very profound spiritual matters. He referred to buried treasures, loans, coins, sheep, seeds, oil, lamps, and daily wages in a vineyard.[6]

If this man was tacky, then Jesus could be considered the same. Mouw paraphrases Patrick Ryan: "It shouldn't surprise us if the Savior who came to ordinary people riding on an ass reveals the Father to some of us in tacky images."[7]

Time and again, the New Testament describes people who encounter God as they are and from where they are. It's no surprise, then, that Jesus would say to a group of fishermen that they are to be those who "fish for people" (Mark 1:17). Jesus regularly uses his contemporary cultural realities to communicate his greatest truths. He was happy to use images from culture, social contexts, and politics if it meant communicating the truth of his kingdom to those who listened. I wonder whether people have considered some of Jesus' theology tacky in his day and age.

A Christian view of revelation—God revealing himself—should rightly recognize that God can speak through whomever God wishes. This is why Christian theologians distinguish between general and special revelation.[8] Special revelation is the knowledge given from God to his covenant people about himself, his will, and his plan. General revelation—or common grace—is knowledge given to everyone. Just like a parent, God has two voices: an "outside voice" that everyone can "hear"—what we can know about God from culture, intellect, experience, creation, sunrises and sunsets, a scientific reading of the universe—and an "inside voice" shared quietly through Scripture with those who trust and love God. Indeed, Christians have always held to the belief that God makes himself known through non-Christian sources. As such, not only *should* we be willing to learn from culture; we *must* learn from it so as to hear God's full revelation to us. Just as John Calvin believed a pagan could receive revelation from God, so too should the Christian eagerly expect God to reveal truth through sources that aren't explicitly "Christian."[9]

The Identity/Relevance Dilemma

In seeking to learn from the cultures we inhabit, there will always be twin dangers of sliding into either syncretism or separation. Syncretism (Greek, *syncretizein*) means to "combine" or "blend" the church's historic teachings and gospel message with some additional cultural, philosophical, or ideological commitment. When the church becomes syncretic, it embraces and embodies the ways and beliefs of the world as part of her witness. Think of fruitcake. Fruitcake is the blending of two very good things— fruit and cake. Yet, if we're honest, their combination becomes, for many of us, something horrific!

Syncretism does not see any difference between biblical truth and popular thinking, philosophy, national or ethnic values, ideology, nationalism, and the like. Syncretism sees Scripture as little more than the product of culture. This theological tendency ends up subsuming Scripture under culture, and in so doing, Scripture loses its prophetic and countercultural witness. Theologian Karl Barth saw syncretism as the thing that kept the German church from confronting the Third Reich. The German church, he believed, had forgotten her call to be a prophet to the state and so became one with the state.[10] When the church marries the present age, someone once told me, she will find herself a widow in the next.

Likewise, neither should the church be sectarian or separatist and pull herself completely away from the world. When the church is sectarian, she disengages from culture and abandons her mission to the world as salt and light, as Jesus commanded (Matthew 5:13–16). By retreating into Christian schools, journals, and institutions—all of which can have profound value—the church can slowly lose her voice within the realm of culture.

The irony of thinkers like Jerome or Tertullian is how often they considered and reflected on the writings of broader culture. Tertullian himself regularly drew on cultural writings from the broader Greco-Roman society to provide illustrations and ideas about Christ—and that's to say nothing of the fact that the biblical text of the New Testament is written in the cultural vernacular of everyday people in a language known as *koine* (or "common") Greek. Even the inspired medium of Scripture refuses to locate God's own divine self-revelation outside the context of real culture and real people in the real world.

The dangerous ditches of syncretism and sectarianism are fleshed out in a book by the late German theologian Jürgen Moltmann titled *The Crucified God*. In this set of reflections on the suffering of Christ, Moltmann discusses the ongoing challenge for the church in the arena of mission—specifically, how the church can be *in* the world but not *of* it.[11] He calls this the "identity-involvement dilemma."[12] At the heart of this predicament is the constant tension the church faces to be present to a broken and hurting world while simultaneously guarding its boundaries of what it will or will not receive.

In Moltmann's perspective, we can become sectarian in our identity and pull away from culture and the system of the world—an act that causes us to lose our prophetic witness within the world of Christ's kingdom, wherein we isolate ourselves, protecting our faith while failing to share the saving message of Christ with the world. Or we can become so immersed in the ways of the world (opting for cultural relevance) that we eventually lose our sense of self as God's people. Often we find ourselves torn between these two tensions. In being wholly immersed in the world, we run the risk of diluting our faith. But in separating from the world, we run the risk of having no people to pass the faith to.

The need to iron out this tension is due to the fact that the Christian movement—like its Jewish forebears—consists of a people called to be a missionary presence in the world. But this call creates a profound awkwardness. For this mission should not strip the people of God of their distinct holiness. Christians in the world will always live in the tension between God's mission and their own holiness. Rodney Stark, in his book *One True God*, makes the case that monotheistic religious traditions are unique in that they are missionary communities. But because of their belief in the one true God, they go into the world to transform it.[13] In faithfulness to God, we are called to go into the world but not be transformed by it. If the call of Christ to his disciples to "go and make disciples of all nations" is true and worthy to be followed (Matthew 28:19), then doing this task with wisdom is critical. We are called to make disciples of Jesus; we are not called to be made into disciples of the world.

Again, a little history. In the 1990s and early 2000s, everything was driving the church toward cultural relevance. In evangelical churches, we were told that a desire to embody the cultural norms of our time should shape our worship gatherings, the way we run the church, and our development of a missional voice in the world. Cultural relevance is indeed a critical component of a church that understands its place in the world. The problem in many of these spaces, however, was the fact that there was no difference between *cultural* relevance and *theological* relevance. Churches that bent over backward to look like the world they sought to reach became prone to reshaping their beliefs to fit the world's needs. We confused *being in* the world with *believing like* the world.

In short, there are boundaries to relevance. The church must embody the culture it finds itself in while seeking to hold faithfully to the witness the church has had for two thousand years. How can one be both theologically sound and culturally sensitive at the same time?[14] This is a tough nut to crack.

Still, perhaps nothing is more important. Scripture itself witnesses to the sophisticated approach taken by the writers of the New Testament toward simultaneous engagement with differentiation from the Greco-Roman world. We know the earliest churches continued to be involved in the life of the culture. We are told that they "continued to meet together in the temple courts" just after Pentecost (Acts 2:46). They continued to engage. But they also differentiated themselves from the world. For instance, the New Testament word for "church" (Greek, *ekklesia*) was borrowed from the surrounding culture. Before the church used this word to describe the gathering of God's people, it was used for a gathering of people seeking the welfare of their city. In fact, twice in Acts 19:39–41, the word *ekklesia* refers to the gathering of civic leaders who are discussing city matters.[15] Originally, the term had zero religious undertones. So we see that the earliest Christians were more than willing to borrow from the broader culture to describe what God was doing among them.

But that is not the entire story. We simultaneously see that the early church rejected some terms to use in speaking of the church. For instance, the ancient concept of the *ruler* (Greek, *archon*) was someone who played a role of authority in civic government. This term was often used to refer to a "synagogue ruler" who gave leadership to Jewish civic centers. Yet, interestingly, the New Testament writers intentionally sidestep such language and speak instead of elders, teachers, shepherds, and the like. There were to be no rulers in the church analogous to the way rulers governed Roman society.[16]

Here we see the church establishing clear boundaries around who they are and who the world is. The earliest Christians adopted the language of *ekklesia* to speak of the church. But not once in the New Testament writings is the word *archon* used to describe the leaders of the church. Clearly, the church saw learning about and from the world as a missional activity.[17] But they did so with discernment.

Edge Species

Christians are a people in-between. During my doctoral studies, I attended a workshop in which a few recent studies on animal life were being discussed. The speaker that day talked about how there are whole categories of species that have adapted to learn how to live in two biozones at once. If a forest was near an ocean, some nearby species would learn how to survive in both biozones. In most cases, they learned to live between these two regions. These are called "edge species." And many different kinds of edge species exist, including grizzly bears, snow leopards, and bald eagles.

Reflecting on these various species, I was struck with the importance of a similar set of skills for the twenty-first-century follower of Jesus. It would be easy to exist in the world alone, hiding in the safe realm of religion. But it would be equally easy to become entirely immersed in the life of the world and forget your identity. The church is, above all, an edge species called by God to simultaneously exist faithfully in the world and for God.

How do we do this? Perhaps one of the most instructive biblical accounts is that of four exiles known as Daniel, Hananiah, Mishael, and Azariah as told in the book of Daniel. Around the year 587 BCE, the Babylonian Empire had conquered the southern kingdom of Judah under the ruthless leadership of King Nebuchadnezzar. The Assyrians—who had previously overwhelmed and conquered the northern kingdom of Israel—had opted to practice intermarriage as a colonial policy. The Assyrians assimilated through forced marriage as a way of weakening family and ancestral ties. Not so the Babylonians, who instead took their captives back to their capital city of Babylon to be assimilated and forced into service of the empire. And so, after conquering

Jerusalem and hearing the news that his father had recently died, Nebuchadnezzar returned to Babylon with three to five thousand of the best and brightest of Israel for assimilation into Babylonian life. These people brought to Babylon were called "exiles."

The book of Daniel is particularly relevant to this conversation because it offers a story of four colonized Jews who found themselves in a dangerous foreign land that did not share their religious or cultural distinctives. It's an ideal vision of how covenant people who love their God are to live in the world but be different from it. The first thing Nebuchadnezzar does is change the names of the four Hebrew men to Babylonian names: Belteshazzar, Shadrach, Meshach, and Abednego. Compelling a change of one's indigenous name serves as a power play to destabilize identity and cultural sense of self. The exiles do not resist this change of their names.

Nor do they resist working for the Babylonian Empire as skilled leaders serving the regime. They "entered the king's service" (Daniel 1:19). These men became useful to the Babylonians because "God gave knowledge and understanding of all kinds of literature and learning. And Daniel could [also] understand visions and dreams of all kinds" (1:17). This reveals that the four exiles opted for a posture toward culture in which they engaged in a noncombative way.

So, on one level, they immersed themselves in the cultural milieu of their exilic experience. Yet they refused other activities. In Daniel 1, the Babylonians tell the Jewish men to eat the Babylonian food at the king's table. This they resist. Given that Jews show the world their sense of identity by means of the way they eat, following the kosher laws, this identity boundary simply cannot be crossed. They request to eat only vegetables and water. And God provides great strength and nourishment to the exiles.

Later, we see a similar point of resistance. In Daniel 3, the king of Babylon demands that the men bow down and worship a statue made in his image. Shadrach, Meshach, and Abednego resist, and we soon find them in a fiery furnace from which God miraculously rescues them. These acts of not defiling themselves with unkosher food and refusing to bow down and worship another god serve as what scholars call "hidden transcripts."[18] These were small but intentional acts of resistance that enabled the exiles to communicate to God, each other, and the world that they were different and set apart.

Notice that these displaced men intentionally resisted in one area but not another. These exiles embodied wise, missional differentiation from Babylon. In fact, along with the book of Ezra, Daniel is the only writing in the Old Testament with extant sections not written in the mother tongue of the ancient Hebrews. Six chapters of Daniel are written in the ancient language of Aramaic, which would have been familiar to many Babylonians. Why? Perhaps it was so these Jews could be a witness to their colonizers. Or perhaps the use of Aramaic was their way of reminding *themselves* that they were not home. Just as many Mennonite Christians in the sixteenth and seventeenth centuries chose to write their records in languages not their own, this may have served as an internal reminder that their true home was somewhere else.[19]

Daniel and his friends are *in* the Babylonian system. But the way they live is a subversive witness against that system. This way of existing places them in the world but puts them at odds with it. That is what exilic faithfulness is all about. Being an exile is like living in spiritual jet lag.[20] While God's covenant people may exist within one time zone, their bodies and spirits are attuned to an entirely different one. Daniel may have been in Babylon, but he was living as though he was still in Jerusalem.

This spiritual jet lag is brilliantly illustrated in the later part of the book of Daniel, when the angel Gabriel comes to Daniel at night. Remember, the temple space in Jerusalem had been destroyed at this point. The sacrifices and daily rituals that Daniel had once known and participated in had ceased. Yet the angel comes to Daniel at "about the time of the *evening sacrifice*" (Daniel 9:21, italics mine). How could that be? The evening sacrifices were no longer happening. Apparently, Daniel and his friends in Babylon were still living on temple time.

This is why guarding one's thinking is of utmost importance for the person who seeks to be faithful to God. "Whatever is true, whatever is noble, whatever is right, whatever is pure, whatever is lovely, whatever is admirable—if anything is excellent or praiseworthy—think about such things," Paul wrote to the Christians in the heart of the Roman Empire at Philippi (Philippians 4:8). Or as the author of Hebrews wrote, "Do not be carried away by all kinds of strange teachings" (Hebrews 13:9). Why? Because even errant thinking can be an exilic experience. We can be "carried off" by it.

Until Christ returns, we exist in Babylon. And we must realize that our thinking and learning can slowly be colonized by the systems of Babylon around us. Being entrenched in this system, our minds can slowly stray from truth. As David writes of being "drawn to what is evil" (Psalm 141:4), our thinking needs to constantly be brought back to God. In other words, we all experience what Gerald May calls the "prodigal mind."[21] Our thinking must return to the living God. If it doesn't, the differences between us and the ways of Babylon will soon disappear.

Control Beliefs

Daniel and his friends were willing to give their time and energy to work for the Babylonian Empire. But they were unwilling to break their kosher laws that guided Jewish eating practice; nor were they willing to bow down in worship to the graven image of Nebuchadnezzar. One lesson Daniel teaches us is that he and his exile friends had theological boundaries that helped them flourish, be a blessing to Babylon, and remain faithful to God. What could help someone like Daniel, and us, engage with our cultural moment while simultaneously setting us apart as witnesses in the world?

Years ago, during a season of pastoral ministry, I was told by a young man in our congregation that he was sensing that Jesus was telling him he was free to leave his wife because she no longer sexually fulfilled him. I was grateful to be invited into such an important conversation. But I also knew this was a monumental moment for this young man. Moments like these in the work of pastoral ministry reveal much about our internal beliefs and what guides and controls our actions in the world.

Fortunately, resting right next to me in my backpack was a copy of the New Testament. I pulled out the sacred writings of Scripture and read out loud what Jesus said about adultery and divorce. I showed him that Jesus could not have told him what he thought he had heard. Why? Because Jesus is consistent. And Jesus' true voice to us would never violate the spoken words of Jesus in Scripture. God's voice, I told him, would never violate God's word.

Without the Bible, we are doomed to make God in our own image. Because of Scripture, anything that leads to spiritual abuse is put in its right place—things like coercion, the sinful misuse of people, and toxic ways of living. As we faithfully engage in the realms of culture, Scripture gives us the boundaries of thought we so desperately need. We need godly bias that shapes our assumptions about truth and the world. Without it, we go wherever culture goes.

We are all biased. We all have assumptions. And that is okay. We need a set of what Christian philosopher Nicholas Wolterstorff calls "control beliefs."[22] And for the Christian, the most consequential control beliefs are the words of Scripture written and inspired to guide and shape life. Scripture is *norma normans*—it serves as the determining norm that "rules over all human opinions, church traditions, church doctrines, creeds, and academic disciplines."[23] As such, the reading of Scripture is what John Wesley called a "compass of thought."[24]

Scripture played a central role in the early church to discern what was of God and what was not. Indeed, we *must* be engaged with culture. But we must do it with careful eyes and hearts. In 1 John 4:1–6, John outlines a series of clear admonitions around who was to be listened to. For John, "Every spirit that does not acknowledge Jesus is not from God" (v. 3). That is, some things should *not* be listened to and received. If anyone or anything denies the reality of Jesus Christ, that voice is not to be trusted.

In the early church, Ignatius argued that whoever does not have a high view of Jesus should not be given weight: "Be deaf, then, to any talk that ignores Jesus Christ, of David's lineage, of Mary; who was really born, ate, and drank; was really persecuted under Pontius Pilate; was really crucified and died."[25]

Without control beliefs, we drift along in whatever direction the currents are going. A number of years ago, I wrote a book proposal for an academic volume based on research I had completed the year before. The publishing board was wildly pleased with the proposal. But there was a catch. They demanded that I include a section on a topic I not only disagreed with but believed to be a violation of a key component of historic Christian ethics. I felt caught. The publisher was ready to offer me a great book contract and even a decent amount of money, but only if I agreed to include writing about something I believed to be entirely contradictory to the Christian witness. I went a different direction.

This experience taught me something integral: Good and true beliefs do not happen accidentally. Still, I'm grateful for this lesson. Experiences like this have the power to teach us the gift of boundaries. We are often incentivized to compromise on things that make Christian conviction Christian. In short, the world would like to colonize our witness. To gain the favor of the world, we contort ourselves to its wants.[26] We gain a hearing, but we lose our voice.

This experience taught me that even in the realm of Christian publishing, I needed a rubric, a set of theological convictions, some control beliefs to guide my decisions. Without them, I would simply accept the publisher's wishes to get a book deal. Being a Christian who holds Scripture in high regard is one of the most difficult and central tasks in our moment. As did Daniel, we will feel pressure both inside and outside the church to abandon what has been revealed in God's written text.

It is interesting to note that by the time the New Testament was written, the nation of Babylon no longer existed. It sat in ruins, having been demolished centuries earlier. Yet when the apostle Peter wrote his first letter, he said it was written "in Babylon" (1 Peter 5:13). Babylon was no longer a place, but it was still a reality. Peter was making a point. To be a Christian today is to live in Babylon as did Daniel. It is always the empire's desire to colonize our learning—to make it their own, to forge it into their image, to make it beastly. How do we resist this and guard our learning unto the Lord?

For those who are exiles in a foreign land, it is vitally important to not allow their thinking to get ahead of God. Paul laid out this very method in his letters: "Do not go beyond what is written" (1 Corinthians 4:6). And by "written," Paul is expressly referring to the sacred text of Scripture. Paul didn't want Christians to go beyond what God had said. This is crucial, given that the serpent consistently wants to take us further than God. This is why Jesus has to tell Satan to "get behind" him (Matthew 16:23). Satan wants to take the lead.

John gives this warning in his second letter: "Anyone who *runs ahead* and does not continue in the teaching of Christ does not have God; whoever continues in the teaching has both the Father and the Son" (2 John 9, italics mine). We need to think. But even our thinking should follow Jesus, not try to get ahead of him.

Plundering the Egyptians

With a set of control beliefs—a deep sense of conviction shaped and forged by the heart and words of Scripture—Christians are able to move freely in whatever context they find themselves in. They become missional agents who transform the world as they go. Like Neo from *The Matrix*, we enter the world to free people from the world. This is one reason Christianity became, in the words of Kurt Aland, "a religion of the city."[27] The spread of Christianity throughout the Roman cities inevitably revitalized them. Rodney Stark described the impact:

Christianity revitalized life in Greco-Roman cities by providing new norms and new kinds of social relationships able to cope with many urgent urban problems. To cities filled with the homeless and impoverished, Christianity offered charity as well as hope. To cities filled with newcomers and strangers, Christianity offered an immediate basis for attachments. To cities filled with orphans and widows, Christianity provided a new and expanded sense of family. To cities torn by violent ethnic strife, Christianity offered a new basis for social solidarity. . . . What [early Christian missionaries] brought was not simply an urban movement, but a *new culture* capable of making life in Greco-Roman cities tolerable.[28]

The earliest Christians went *to* culture to transform it. And they got this idea through reading Scripture. It tells story after story of individuals who learn from the culture around them. The creation story in Genesis uses the word *Elohim* for God, which is not from the Hebrew vocabulary. The biblical authors opt to use a non-Hebrew word to speak about their covenant God. Israel learns from the Egyptians (Isaiah 19:11–13), the Edomites (Jeremiah 49:7), and the Phoenicians (Zechariah 9:2). The capacity for human wisdom is narrated in explicit form in Job 28:1–11. The New Testament letter of Jude alludes to the noncanonical book *Testament of Moses* (Jude 9).[29] And we even see that Paul quotes (approvingly, mind you) pagan philosophers in his preaching of the gospel in Acts 17:28.

Paul regularly quoted the poets and philosophers to make his points. His use of the word *euangelion* ("good news") for the gospel shows that he is willing to borrow Roman categories to speak about Christian realities. Moreover, when Paul recounts his own conversion story—which he does three times in Acts—he mentions in his final account that Jesus had said to him on the road to Damascus, "Saul, Saul, why do you persecute me? It is hard for you to kick against the goads" (Acts 26:14). Here, Paul quotes Jesus as saying something not recorded in Paul's conversion story in Acts 9. It turns out that Jesus is quoting a familiar saying in the Greek world dating back to a fifth-century play by a Greek playwright named Euripides.[30] Apparently, even Jesus quoted pagan playwrights to communicate the gospel to Saul as he traveled to kill Christians in Damascus. Considering Jesus likely spoke at least Greek, Aramaic, Latin, and Hebrew, he was quite the cultured man. Given this reality, are humans *really* supposed to separate from culture entirely?

That Christianity embraced culture speaks to why it spread as much as it did. In his book *Christian Worship and Its Cultural Setting*, Frank Senn argues that Christianity spread so effectively because it adapted to whatever culture it came to. The same could not be said of Islam. The difference? Islam only spread when Muslim culture and language spread—which is seen in the fact that the Qur'an must be rendered only in Arabic. The Christian Scriptures, however, were permitted to be translated.[31] In this sense, Christianity has proven to be missionally flexible wherever it goes.

In the early church, this question was taken up by the fourth-century bishop Augustine. In his *Teaching Christianity (De Doctrina Christiana)*, he uses the illustration of the Israelites. As they come out of Egypt, the Egyptians give them plunder and booty—gold and resources. Heading into the wilderness to worship God, the people of Israel arrive at Mount Sinai, where they will spend one whole year. Yet just a few weeks following their time in enslavement, the people make a golden calf to worship. What do they make the calf out of? The gold the Egyptians had given them. For Augustine, this biblical moment exposed a key insight for how to learn from pagans. It is one thing to "plunder the Egyptians"; it is another to worship like the Egyptians do— or worship the gifts the Egyptians had given.[32]

Learning from the world should be a normative part of the Christian life. As God did with his people in the wilderness, he desires to provide for us as freed people who are wandering toward the promised land. But to receive gifts from our surrounding culture requires a deep humility to not misuse them in ways never intended.

Jesus spent three years walking with his disciples. As he did, were they aware that they were being transformed? Jesus came to be *with* the disciples. One of the most important ideas I received from my doctoral supervisor, Dr. Mark Cartledge, was his deep belief that the church is to play a similar "being with" role in the world. Just as Jesus transformed the disciples by walking with them, so the church helps to transform the world by walking alongside it. When the church walks with the world, it has its most profound effect.[33]

Eight

Learning from Enemies

"Just as the physical needs of the body cannot be met by a continuous series of snacks," writes Lesslie Newbigin in *The Good Shepherd*, "so your mental and spiritual needs cannot be met by a continual series of little devotional books, sermons and booklets."[1] When I read these words for the first time, they seemed to leap off the page. Up to that point in life, my reading diet included little more than snacking. I didn't know how to feast—let alone where to find one.

Reading is a major part of my life. And not just reading, but reading well and reading deeply. To serve this task, I eventually developed a system for reading—a menu, if you will—that includes five different kinds of books I discipline myself to read: acquaintances, neighbors, friends, lovers, and enemies. What are these? Here's a quick introduction to my reading taxonomy that ensures I'm always eating a hearty meal and not just snacking.

An *acquaintance* is a book you picked up along the way but discover just as quickly you can put down. You may bump into an acquaintance. But you needn't give them more attention than required. Given the sheer number of good books available to read, it is crucial that you become as skilled at putting some of them down as you are at picking them up.

A *neighbor* is a book you are required to know in light of your responsibilities, position, or scholarship. If you're a student, this is an assigned textbook or perhaps a book your peer group or leadership team is working through for continuing education in your line of work. Nobody gets to choose their neighbors, but you have to live next to them and learn from them regardless.

A *friend* is a book you enjoy. This is a pleasure read. For me, this includes reading the works of George MacDonald, a newspaper, or a devotional from a favorite theologian or thinker. In short, a friend is someone I enjoy being with.

And a *lover*—well, that's the book or author you return to over and over to shape you in the most intimate of ways. These are people and writings you simply can't put down but must come back to time and time again.

Then there are *enemies*—the books or authors with whom you disagree.

The thinking behind this admittedly neurotic system is simple: Reading is for more than mere enjoyment. We read because we love. C. S. Lewis said that part of the reason reading is difficult is that it takes our attention off ourselves and puts it on another. In this way, reading is the art of paying attention to another. Lewis wrote, "One of the chief operations of art is to remove our gaze from that mirrored face, to deliver us from that solitude . . . entering fully into the opinions, and therefore also the attitudes, feelings, and total experience, of other men."[2] Reading takes us into someone else's world. The work of reading beckons us out of ourselves to learn from and love someone on *their* terms. This is a work of love—to enter someone else's world, as Jesus did, so love may manifest. "Reading," Jean Rhys wisely reflects, "makes immigrants of us all."[3]

Reading makes us travelers in other people's minds. I like reading friends. I love reading lovers. I have to read neighbors. But I do not enjoy reading enemies. These are books written by someone you know from the outset you don't agree with. The enemy does not say what you want them to say. They take you into a way of thinking you would not likely visit on your own. They challenge your assumptions. And they push your buttons.

For the Christian, this raises an important issue: Does reading your enemies give them too much power in your life? Should we read those we disagree with? And can they spur us on to be more like Christ?

There's significant debate to be had about this—one I force my students to wrestle with in one of my courses. Should we, for example, read Adolf Hitler's *Mein Kampf*, an antisemitic rant written from prison outlining what the future dictator longed to do once he got into power? Should Hitler's evil thoughts be read? Normally, the class is torn over this issue. Some think the book should never be read. Others think it should be burned—a common feature, ironically, of the Nazi state Hitler gave rise to. I suggest that our ignorance of the enemy can have the opposite impact from what we expect—that *not* reading our enemies gives them power.

How? When the evilest ideas are ignored, our intellectual immune system weakens. And given there is no *new* bad idea—only rewarmed ones—wouldn't it be wise to keep our minds sharp by challenging them? It is nearly impossible to dismantle a bad argument if you haven't thought it through. That's to say nothing of the fact that canceling someone's ideas or thoughts usually fails to exterminate them; instead it can send them underground to grow stronger. In the world of immunology, inoculation may defeat a globe-transforming illness. But when it disappears and our bodies no longer have to face it, we are more susceptible to it when it returns. Spending years in the ruts of intellectual familiarity can undermine one's ability to cultivate deep, faithful critical thinking skills. It keeps us from maturing. Sure, living in a bubble may be safe, but it's exceptionally bad for having a healthy intellectual immune system.

An "enemy," then, can be one of many things. In this instance, I want to broadly define an enemy as "someone with whom we disagree." This may include a true enemy, such as Hitler. And it may include a friendly enemy, such as someone who disagrees with your thinking in the name of seeking to sharpen your thinking. In one instance, the enemy is actually a person who could be considered dangerous or hostile. But in another, the enemy is someone whose thought or critique can help sharpen or correct our own. While they may be very different from each other, they both hold a similar power for us—they can help us become stronger.

This debate became a pivotal question in the early church. Should Christians read the writings of the heretics whose teachings went against those of the apostles? Surprisingly, the early church held that the teachings of the heretics should be rejected—but still listened to. In *On Christian Doctrine*, Augustine says truth can from time to time be found among the pagans. The medieval theologian Thomas Aquinas argued that divergent viewpoints had the power to help us inch toward theological truth. He believed we could even learn from those who disagreed with us.

It's clear that those in the church who wrestled with the theology of the heretics first engaged their teachings. Burning the books of the heretics, ironically, didn't incinerate their ideas. Rather, they were allowed to fester and grow under the surface. This gave them more power.

Engaging Our Enemies

As a writer, I've found this principle of engaging our enemies to be extremely important. Over time, I've learned to be more attentive to the voices of good faith critics who disagree with my thinking. They often have something to say that can help me sharpen my own thinking. Not only is this something to put up with, but it's also something I desperately need. For the Christian, learning from an enemy isn't the same as agreeing with an enemy. An enemy can sharpen us through disagreement.

Social scientists tell us that when we are around people who think the exact same way we do, we tend to become more radicalized in our beliefs. That is, being in a homogenous community increases the chance that we develop false beliefs. This is called the "law of group polarization." And it can create a dangerous environment where thinking that holds us accountable is not permitted. As we spend time only with those who agree with us, our beliefs tend to become increasingly extreme and absent of accountability.

Of course, balance is needed. It is not wise to read *only* our enemies. But listening to those who disagree with us should be a normal part of our intellectual diet. By engaging our enemies, we put ourselves in the position of being made sharper. This is well illustrated by the relationship between two former Supreme Court justices—Antonin Scalia and Ruth Bader Ginsburg. Ideologically and politically, these two were as far apart as two could be. But over the years, they cultivated a friendship that shaped them both. To read Scalia's book *Scalia Speaks* and hear him speak in glowing terms of his legal enemy is not only countercultural; it is inspiring. It is actually possible that by learning from our enemies' ideas, we can better clarify our own. So much so that Ginsburg wrote the foreword to his book.[4]

Our enemies may have something to teach us, but to listen and learn from them is entirely counterintuitive to us. We often do one of two things with our enemies—ignore them or seek their demise. For one thing, acknowledging our enemies can sometimes make us look bad by comparison. When I lecture through the book of Exodus, there is always a hearty discussion around whether the Israelites really were brought out of Egypt. There is some decent scholarly debate around this. How could it be possible for nearly a million Hebrews to leave Egypt without mention of this in the official records of the ancient Egyptians? I put myself in the shoes of the Egyptians. They have a valid reason to ignore such an exodus. How bad would it make them look to admit that a whole subjugated people group escaped overnight into the wilderness? They had good reason to conceal such a defeat. Regimes don't want word getting out when their enemies get the best of them—so they ignore their enemies to make themselves look better.

We also fail to notice our enemies when we surround ourselves only with friends. It is easy to love people just like ourselves, isn't it? But this kind of love is shallow and does not transform anyone. In his book *The Wisdom of Each Other*, Eugene Peterson shares a parable about a young man named Gunnar who finds a new church. Now that Gunnar is deciding if he will join the church, he says he is struggling to connect with people there. Peterson pens the pastor's response:

You say that you have almost nothing in common with these people. But isn't that just the point? *You* have nothing in common with them; but *God* does. This just happens to be the way that God goes about making a kingdom, pulling all sorts and conditions of people together and then patiently, mercifully, and graciously making something of them. What he obviously does not do is pre-select people who have an aptitude for getting along well and enjoying the same things. Of course you don't have much in common with them. The church is God's thing; not yours.[5]

Gunnar's desire to be around people he has much in common with is not unique. We would all rather be with people just like ourselves. But when we do that, it keeps us from growing up.

Other times, we make ourselves too busy to listen to our enemies. Who has time to listen to enemies when there isn't even enough time to listen to friends and family? The busyness that controls our lives can keep us from spending time in the presence of our enemies. No doubt, our lack of time keeps us from engaging in ideas that make us uncomfortable. We don't know how to pay attention to our enemies—to say nothing of actually reading their ideas and listening to their reflections.

When we can't just ignore our enemies but are forced to confront them, our natural reaction is to desire their demise. That is, rather than desiring to see our enemies transformed, we would rather see them destroyed. There is no better illustration of this than in the ancient story of the Hebrew prophet Jonah. First, he runs away from any possible contact with the Ninevites who have just destroyed his homeland. Then after encountering again God's command to go to them, he makes his journey to the land of his enemies. It is only after having seen his enemies receive God's mercy and love that he spends the final chapter of his book under a tree spouting out anger at God that God would have the audacity to love his enemies. Not only is our impulse to run away from our enemies; in many instances it represents the opposite of God's call on our lives. We aren't to run from Nineveh; God often calls us to run to it.

Noticing Our Enemies

To move toward our enemies offers a very different posture toward them than we are used to seeing. In the movies, enemies are meant to be killed. In politics, the enemy is to be ideologically attacked. In popular culture, the enemy is to be canceled. But there is another way. In the ancient wisdom of Proverbs 24, the people of Israel are commanded by God, "Do not gloat when your enemy falls; when they stumble, do not let your heart rejoice, or the LORD will see and disapprove and turn his wrath away from them" (vv. 17–18). We are commanded to never celebrate the fall of an enemy.

In the Hasidic tradition of Judaism, it is told that after the Israelites were saved from Egypt and the Egyptians were drowned in the Red Sea, the angels in heaven were celebrating the death of their enemies. But one of the angels asked out loud, "Where is God? Why isn't God here celebrating?" Michael, the archangel, answered, "God is not here because he is off by himself weeping. You see, many thousands drowned today."[6]

Of course, this exchange isn't found in Scripture. But it remains remarkable that a people formed by Scripture would imagine God this way—a God who *grieves* when his own enemies perish. What is found in Scripture are Jesus' clear teachings to his disciples that they are to love and pray for their enemies:

"You have heard that it was said, 'Love your neighbor and hate your enemy.' But I tell you, love your enemies and pray for those who persecute you, that you may be children of your Father in heaven. He causes his sun to rise on the evil and the good, and sends rain on the righteous and the unrighteous. If you love those who love you, what reward will you get? Are not even the tax collectors doing that?" (Matthew 5:43–46)

For those who would be his disciples, Jesus gives two express commands: Love your enemy and pray for your persecutor. Why? So you may be the children of God. Jesus then says that rain is given both to the righteous and to the unrighteous. The psychological impact on the disciples—who were actively being persecuted by Rome when these words were given—was likely earth-shattering. Love your enemies well. And remember that God cares for them as much as he does for you.

One simple way to love our enemies is to give them our attention. The Jewish philosopher Emmanuel Levinas—who was imprisoned during World War II—said that to be able to see something of God in their enemy is one of the unique attributes of a truly formed human: "To be able to see in the face of the other, in the face of those who would try to kill me, in the face of the criminal, the face of God, this is the hardest challenge of the religious enterprise."[7]

This kind of posture toward our enemies may make us uncomfortable. And rightfully so. It doesn't make sense to want to see our enemies flourish or experience love. Especially when it comes to our real enemies, we want them exposed and destroyed. In his book *The Constitution of Knowledge*, Jonathan Rauch says that the social environment of tribalism doesn't allow us to love the enemy.[8]

We don't want to teach our enemies, learn from them, or even love them. Rather, our goal is to be "seeking to demoralize" them at every turn.[9] We do not want the best for our enemies. We want them to be removed from power—to be socially, politically, and sometimes literally destroyed. We saw this when Hillary Clinton referred to conservatives as "deplorables." And we saw it in a speech when Donald Trump Jr. mentioned that the whole "turn the cheek" teaching of Jesus was no longer valid. Politics is now built on the destruction of the enemy at all costs. If our enemies, borrowing Trump Jr., are using war tactics, then so should we:

> We've been playing T-ball for half a century while they're playing hardball and cheating. Right? We've turned the other cheek, and I understand, sort of, the biblical reference—I understand the mentality—*but it's gotten us nothing.* Okay? *It's gotten us nothing* while we've ceded ground in every major institution in our country."[10]

This brings us back to our earlier distinction between real enemies and friendly enemies. There are times, to be sure, when learning from an enemy is a means of undermining what they are seeking to do. This is often the case with real enemies. We don't learn from them because they are good. We learn from them to overcome them. In his book *The Art of War*, Chinese military leader Sun Tzu outlined the importance of engaging one's enemies. His entire military strategy—which would have great implications on the global stage—was built on first learning from an enemy before you could defeat them.

The revered Indian activist Mahatma Gandhi would eventually bring an end to generations-long British colonial rule of his own country. Gandhi is best known for his practice of nonviolence (*ahimsa*). But it was his study of one of his greatest enemies, General Reginald Dyer, who was responsible for the Jallianwala Bagh Massacre in 1919, that helped him understand how to resist him. Nelson Mandela, too, used his time in prison to study the tactics of those who oversaw apartheid in South Africa.

But there are other times when we learn from friendly enemies, not to undermine what they are doing, but to better them and ourselves. In this instance, we enfranchise this enemy into our lives so that everyone can be transformed. This can be seen, writes Doris Kearns Goodwin, in how Abraham Lincoln would intentionally hire those he had defeated in the presidential election so that he could surround himself with people who thought differently.[11] Rather than banish his enemies from the political system, Lincoln hired them to make his presidency stronger.

Scripture is replete with examples of God's people paying attention to and learning from their enemies. David, during his years of exile under the ruthless rule of Saul, spent his time studying and understanding the man who sought his blood. Even the fact that the New Testament gives us details about Judas Iscariot assumes that we are to learn from the enemies of Christ.

In the context of the early church, there are only two humans mentioned in the Apostles' Creed other than Jesus—Mary, the mother of Jesus, and Pontius Pilate, the enemy of Jesus. No other human is mentioned in the Creed—not even Peter or Paul. The earliest Christians experienced tremendous cultural and political pressure to abandon their confession of Jesus as Lord. In this context, it is critical to note that part of a healthy theology and orthodoxy is the remembrance of your enemies. The Apostles' Creed remembers even the enemies of God.

Enemies in Our Mind

Up until now, we have focused largely on how enemies can strengthen us. But there's another side—how our love of our enemies actually transforms them. Jesus was, in the words of biblical scholar Robert Funk, the "consummate party animal."[12] He is always leaving one meal and going to another. And one of the distinctive marks of these meals is that Jesus often gets in trouble for them.

Craig Blomberg's compelling examination of the eating habits of Jesus explores how Jesus transcended moral and cleanliness boundaries of the first century to create space for the people who were perceived to be the unworthy people of society—sinners, tax collectors, and women. Rather than "othering" or dismissing these kinds of people, Jesus ate with them. And it worked. His method was built on transformation by means of acceptance.[13] Jesus changed the world by showing us a way to share food with people who were perceived as outsiders.

We can see in the writings of Paul that in just a few decades, the Christian community had become a place where social enemies were sharing meals in a united spirit. Men and women, children and adults, slaves and enslavers, Jews and Gentiles— all were sharing meals together. The second-century Christian apologist Justin Martyr's early writings confirm that the meal was where hatred toward enemies fell apart. This acceptance of enemies became one of the features of the early church. Justin wrote, "Then we hated one another and murdered one another. . . . Now, after the appearing of Christ, we eat at the same table, and we pray for our enemies, and try to persuade those who unjustly hate."[14]

In fact, the preaching of the early church centered on that

very thing. The most quoted verse in the early church was "Love your enemies." It was quoted some twenty-eight times by ten different authors in the first three hundred years of the church. No other texts were preached on more than those that talked of the love of enemies.[15]

This ethic of love toward the perceived or real enemy shaped some of the most important movements in the modern world. Dietrich Bonhoeffer—when the Third Reich was rising—wrote extensively about what he called "enemy love."[16] Borrowing on this same tradition, Martin Luther King Jr. believed the only way one could truly transform their enemy was to empathize with them—sitting and hearing about their experience in the world. His ideas in *Strength to Love* about the love of the enemy are some of the most powerful notions that spoke into the racial tensions of the twentieth century and gave people of color a voice.[17] The work of reconciliation does not come by dismissing or othering the enemy; it comes, often, by embracing them. This is what the cross is—the embrace of the enemy.[18] While we were still enemies, Christ came and redeemed us.

Jesus made his identity known by loving his enemies, but we tend to make our identity known by rejecting our enemies. We find our own sense of identity and community in who we denounce as enemies. That is, we define ourselves in terms of who we are not like, leading us to become prideful. Enemies remind us of what we are *not*—a spirit exemplified in the Pharisee who prayed, "God, I thank you that I am not like other people— robbers, evildoers, adulterers—or even like this tax collector. I fast twice a week and give a tenth of all I get" (Luke 18:11–12).

Sadly, our nonstop access to social media allows us to identify and scope out our enemies so as to soothe ourselves by proclaiming who we are *not*. Too often, our enemies become the thing we use to inflate our own ego and sense of self-satisfaction. Philosopher James K. A. Smith hauntingly describes the power that things like Facebook and Instagram have in our lives:

> Now we turn to these devices over and over again looking for that peculiar joy of late modernity: the joy of outrage. The delight we take in recognizing what is detestable. The twisted bliss of offense. The haughty thrill of being aghast at the latest transgression. We can't believe he said *that*, and we secretly can't wait for it to happen again. Like love's negative, the joy of outrage is expansive: it only grows when it is shared.[19]

This sense of shared outrage becomes our identity. Of course, this emotional display does nothing to change our enemies—or ourselves. We only manage to give them emotional leverage over our own peace. Again, turning to Martin Luther King Jr., it is at the point that we seek to destroy our enemies that we do our greatest damage. In his famous "Loving Your Enemies" sermon, Martin Luther King Jr. wrote these words:

> Another way that you love your enemy is this: When the opportunity presents itself for you to defeat your enemy, that is the time which you must not do it. There will come a time, in many instances, when the person who hates you most, the person who has misused you most, the person who has gossiped about you most, the person who has spread false rumors about you most, there will come a time when you will have an opportunity to defeat that person. It might be in terms of a recommendation for a job; it might be in terms of helping that person to make some move in life. That's the time you must do it. That is the meaning of love. In the final analysis, love is not

this sentimental something that we talk about. It's not merely an emotional something. Love is creative, understanding goodwill for all men. It is the refusal to defeat any individual. When you rise to the level of love, of its great beauty and power, you seek only to defeat evil systems. Individuals who happen to be caught up in that system, you love, but you seek to defeat the system.[20]

In his letter to the Colossians, Paul talks about the person who has been sinning against God. Because of their sin, this person, Paul says, has become an enemy in their own mind (Colossians 1:21). As a result of sin, we increasingly separate ourselves from God and can't imagine there would be enough grace for us when, in all reality, Christ is ready at a moment's notice to embrace enemies who are adopted by God's love. Our sin does not keep us from God, as we assume it does. Rather, our unwillingness to receive and experience the mercy of God is what keeps us from God.

If, indeed, people are enemies in their minds, then being able to learn from them entails a revolutionized understanding of them in our minds. In short, we have to begin to think remarkably differently about them.

Fear, Love, and Honor

Learning from an enemy is important, but it is also dangerous. We need a paradigm to think about it. In his letter to the churches scattered throughout the Roman Empire, Peter gives some lasting wisdom for how to live in a world of enemies: "Show proper respect to everyone, love the family of believers, fear God, honor the emperor" (1 Peter 2:17). In one jam-packed sentence, Peter gives four commands, one right after the other.

What is he doing here? He is giving exiled Christians throughout the Roman Empire a framework for thinking about how to engage the Babylon they live in. Note that two of these commands are directly suited to how we engage with our Christian identity ("fear God" and "love the family of believers"). The other two have to do with how we engage with our civic and social identity in the world ("show proper respect to everyone" and "honor the emperor").

Peter appears to be outlining a hierarchy of priorities. Clearly, "fear God" is the strongest verb used in this sentence. Next in priority is "love the family of believers." "Respect everyone" and "honor the emperor" are the final priorities.[21] Our first commandment is to, above all, fear God and keep his commandments. This is why the prophet Daniel gets in trouble only when the king says he must "fear" and "worship" him. This is unacceptable for one of God's covenant persons. Second, we are commanded to give of ourselves to serve the brothers and sisters we walk alongside in the way of Jesus. Third, we should give honor to everyone, including the emperor who wanted Christians banished or killed. Peter is saying Christians must honor their enemies.

In the realm of discipleship, whenever this order (fear, love, and honor) is rearranged, there are tragic consequences in the Christian community. When love for neighbor and stranger is placed above love for God, we end up creating a social service organization that is no longer the church devoted to the worship of Jesus Christ. But placing love for neighbor and honor of people under the fear of the Lord provides a road map for knowing how to act. Our first call is to obey Christ. Under that, and with that as our priority, we can love people in a way that brings life.

How do we honor an enemy? We can begin by representing them well and rightly. Often we find it strategic to represent our enemies in the worst light possible. We present them as weaker or less intelligent than they actually are, and we spar with straw men—putting words in our enemies' mouths or engaging only the worst of their arguments to try to make ourselves look smarter. But a Christian should not do this. We shouldn't strawman our enemies; we should steelman them! We should seek to give the most charitable hearing to the people we disagree with, finding their best arguments and wrestling with those.

Next, we don't seek to demolish our enemies; rather, we seek to demolish their arguments. In doing so, we create the possibility of winning them over. Honor does not misrepresent; it represents accurately. As Alan Jacobs writes, "One of the classic ways to do this is to seek out the best—the smartest, most sensible, most fair-minded representatives of the positions you disagree with."[22] Wouldn't we want our enemies to do the same for us? The act of honoring everyone must include, at its foundation, a willingness to speak with respect toward those who are not in the room with us.

This posture of honor also must include choosing not to be offended. As Jesus died on the cross, he asked his Father, "Forgive them, for they do not know what they are doing" (Luke 23:34). Similarly, when Stephen (the first martyr in the church) is killed, he echoes the same sentiment: "Lord, do not hold this sin against them" (Acts 7:60). Neither Jesus nor Stephen offers direct forgiveness. They don't see themselves as the primary ones being offended. They are peacemakers—children of God (Matthew 5:9). In their darkest moment, they understand that the Father is the one truly being offended, the one who truly needs to offer forgiveness. A mature person does not see a disagreement with an enemy as a "me versus them" problem.

Rather, God is at the center, and we are on the periphery. This is what Dallas Willard had in mind when he said that the sign of a truly mature person is "whether one spontaneously responds to one's enemies with love."[23]

The possible trajectory of dishonoring our enemies can be seen clearly in the Sermon on the Mount. Jesus first says that "anyone who is angry with a brother or sister will be subject to judgment." Then anyone who says, "*Raca*," will be "answerable to the court." And finally, anyone who says, "You fool!" will be "in danger of the fire of hell" (Matthew 5:22–23). The word *raca* was a term of profound disregard. Dallas Willard writes:

> The Aramaic term *raca* was current in Jesus' day to express contempt for someone and to mark out him or her as contemptible. It may have originated from the sound one makes to collect spittle from the throat in order to spit. In anger I want to hurt you. In contempt, I don't care whether you are hurt or not. Or at least so I say. You are not worth consideration one way or the other.[24]

The progression is undeniable. What begins with anger soon moves to disdain and eventually becomes a dismissive spirit. When we arrive at this place—even as it relates to enemies—we should know we may be on the path to hell. In this way, an enemy not loved can greatly harm our own journey.

Subversive Learners

At present, many people in the broader culture lack the capacity to talk to anyone unless there is consistent agreement. This failure of imagination spells the downfall of a nation. I once had an idea of starting an underground club where people from all around the city could come under the cloak of night and do the most subversive of activities—say what they actually think. In a world that cancels anyone who thinks differently than they do, this could be a most prophetic act. In my dream, this place would be called a "speakeasy." Silly as it may be, we must begin to cultivate an environment where we can listen to and engage those whose thinking is diametrically opposed to our own.

Engaging with our enemies through the use of carefully chosen words can transform them. Consider the story of Daryl Davis. A Black man, Davis is famous for doing something unthinkable— befriending members of the Ku Klux Klan. In these surprising relationships, Davis goes out of his way to learn the histories and stories of those who hate him because of his skin color. Over time, these friendships change his enemies. Davis's famous testimony includes showing audiences the world over photos of him holding the KKK robes of people who left the Klan through his friendships with them. By learning from and engaging in conversation with his enemies, Davis changes them.[25]

Another example of the power of learning from an enemy can be found near the turn of the twentieth century when a revival broke out in Topeka, Kansas, under the leadership of a man named Charles Parham. The news of this fresh outpouring of the Holy Spirit spread quickly, and Parham's newfound fame took him to Houston, Texas, where he taught from the Bible.

It was not permitted for people of color to sit inside the class where Parham lectured in 1901. Sitting in the hallway was a Black man named William Seymour. As Seymour listened, he heard a fresh teaching about the Holy Spirit that would transform his life forever. Energized by this new experience, Seymour went to Los Angeles to preach. Under his influence, what began as a small prayer gathering grew and grew until it became what we know to be global Pentecostalism.

Parham, who had close ties to the Ku Klux Klan, resented that a Black man would lead a revival, so he traveled to Los Angeles to try to commandeer the movement. Seymour would not let him. This was not a movement of a man; it was a movement of God. And no man could take it from God.[26]

It is ironic that Seymour received the teaching about the Holy Spirit that would give birth to the Pentecostal movement from a man who hated him because of the color of his skin. It is all the more ironic that global Pentecostalism has done much to mitigate centuries of racial pain and oppression by giving the same experience of the Spirit to people who are very different. It would see some of the greatest healing between Black and White churches in all of American history.

It turns out, learning from an enemy can be profoundly subversive . . . and transformative.

Conclusion

Even as this conclusion is being penned, the news is full of economic downturns, military breakouts in various parts of the world, an upcoming election that promises to be painfully divisive, and mass shootings. In moments like this—when everything seems to be falling apart—is there really a need to cultivate the art of teachability? During World War II, C. S. Lewis took up this very question. Europe was descending into great chaos and bloodshed. When society is no longer stable, Lewis asked, why should we continue to go to university? Or be learners? "Is it not," Lewis preached in a sermon, "like fiddling while Rome burns?"

That sermon, titled "Learning in War-Time," offers a clear and poignant argument for why learning is *always* important: "Human life has always been lived on the edge of a precipice. Human culture has always had to exist under the shadow of something infinitely more important than itself. If men had postponed the search for knowledge and beauty until they were secure, the search would never have begun."[1] For Lewis, human history has always had plenty of impending reasons not to enter a life of learning. In fact, he seems to argue, if we wait for a perfect time, we will never start the process.

Opening ourselves to becoming teachable people is not

something we do just to get a new job, make more money, or gain a good reputation. We don't do it to get something; we do it because it forges in us a Christlike character that shapes us over a lifetime. Becoming teachable through the yoke of Christ is God's way of healing the fracture of the fall. In his *Of Education*, John Milton made the case that learning was one of the ways God heals a world marred by sin:

> The end then of learning is to repair the ruins of our first parents by regaining to know God aright, and out of that knowledge to love him, to imitate him, to be like him, as we may the nearest by possessing our souls of true virtue, which being united to the heavenly grace of faith makes up the highest perfection.[2]

As we come to a conclusion, I think about my job as a teacher. I spend my life delivering lectures, mentoring students, and entrusting wisdom and knowledge to my students. I love my job. Still, ever since becoming a professor, I've felt a distinct sense of discomfort with Jesus' command, "Nor are you to be called 'teacher,' for you have one teacher, the Christ" (Matthew 23:10 NET). This is a particularly difficult command to honor when your paycheck depends on breaking it. I am a teacher. It is my job. What do I make of Jesus telling a teacher that they are not to be called a teacher?

Throughout this book, we established that God is our ultimate teacher, and that as part of our loving him, he will send a series of surprising people to help shape us into Christlikeness—people like enemies, strangers, children, parents, and the like. God, the teacher, uses the most extraordinary people and things to make us into the kind of people he wants us to be. But it is God who is the teacher.

And it is God who accompanies us on the journey of learning. Noah benShea, in his book *Jacob the Baker*, tells of a teacher who takes his student out into the dark woods. He then blows out the one light by which they could see. Consumed by fear, the student asks if the teacher is going to leave him in the woods all alone with no way of seeing anything. The teacher assures him that he won't. Rather, the teacher is leaving him so he can learn to search for the light all on his own.[3]

A very important lesson is hidden in benShea's parable. A good teacher wants their student to learn to become their own person. There is wisdom in this. But the Christian story of the aim of teaching has a twist on benShea's account. The goal of the Christian life is not a life of independence in which we need God less and less; rather, its goal is a maturity that is birthed from increased dependence on the Teacher to lead us and guide us into all truth. Christian learning is not the journey of needing God less and less; it's the journey of leaning in to need God more and more as our Teacher.

So then what do I do with Jesus' command? I still call myself a teacher, and my students still call me their teacher. And my paycheck still says I'm a teacher. But this command of Jesus changes the way I think about the journey of learning. Each semester, the university gives me a student worker, known as a teacher assistant. Their task is to help me do the work of teaching. Their work can range from grading papers, organizing activities, ensuring that the course website is running smoothly, proctoring exams, and carrying out other essential duties. I couldn't do my work without them. But they also recognize that they are not the teacher. As many of us have learned, there is nothing worse than the TA who thinks they are the teacher.

Here's the truth though—I'm not the teacher either; I'm just a TA. We all are. As is every single one of those people who find their way into our lives to teach us something—the stranger, the enemy, the parent, the child, the culture, the dead, the expert. Every one of them. Our primary teacher is our God. When Christ is the ultimate teacher, then we get to take our humble place in serving his agenda in this world. Lord knows, there's nothing worse than a TA who forgets their place.

"The student is not above the teacher," Jesus once taught, "but everyone who is fully trained will be like their teacher" (Luke 6:40). The goal, then, for disciples of Jesus is not to get more information from the teacher.

The goal is to become like him.

Acknowledgments

A few words of gratitude. I'm grateful to the Society of Professional Christian Educators (SPCE) for inviting me in October 2023 to give a lecture on intergenerational intelligence—a talk that generally framed the chapter on being taught by our parents. A big thanks as well to the *Journal of Spiritual Formation and Soul Care* for allowing me to reproduce some of my own writing in the chapter on being taught by the dead.

Notes

Introduction

1. See Walter Ciszek and Daniel Flaherty, *He Leadeth Me: An Extraordinary Testament of Faith* (San Francisco: Ignatius, 1995), 19–20.
2. Dallas Willard, *The Allure of Gentleness: Defending the Faith in the Manner of Jesus* (New York: HarperOne, 2015), 3.
3. Madeleine L'Engle, *An Acceptable Time* (New York: Square Fish, 1989), 86.
4. Christopher J. H. Wright, *The Message of Jeremiah* (Downers Grove, IL: InterVarsity, 2014), 51.
5. Theologians call this impact of sin on our minds the "noetic effects of sin." For a primer, peruse John Webster, *Holiness* (Grand Rapids: Eerdmans, 2003).
6. On this "veil," see Acts 9:9–19; 2 Corinthians 3:13–16.
7. Including but not limited to Tertullian, Augustine, Anselm, Thomas Aquinas, C. S. Lewis, Dorothy Sayers, Mark Noll, Os Guinness, George Marsden, James Sire, Richard Middleton, Richard Neuhaus, and Nancy Pearcey.
8. Such as when D. A. Carson (the prolific Reformed theologian) recognized a graduate student's work as superior to his own: "If it is any encouragement, increasing years make one increasingly careful. They are also teaching me, slowly, to change my mind and acknowledge when I am shown to be in error" (*Exegetical Fallacies*, 2nd ed. [Grand Rapids: Baker Academic, 1996], 52).

9. Lewis A. Drummond, *Spurgeon: Prince of Preachers* (Grand Rapids: Kregel, 1992), 101.

10. Brighde Mullins, "Those Who Can, Do," in *Actor's Choice: Monologues for Women*, ed. Erin Detrick (New York: Playscripts, 2008), 128.

Chapter 1: Learning How to Learn

1. See Peter J. Casarella, ed., *Cusanus: The Legacy of Learned Ignorance* (Washington, DC: Catholic University of America Press, 2006).

2. Timothy Gloege, "#ItsNotUs: Being Evangelical Means Never Having to Say You're Sorry," Religion Dispatches, January 3, 2018, https://religiondispatches.org/itsnotus-being-evangelical-means-never-having-to-say-youre-sorry/.

3. See Richard Carrier's consistent claim that Christianity is irrational and anti-intellectual ("A Primer on Christian Anti-Intellectualism," *Richard Carrier Blogs*, June 1, 2022, www.richardcarrier.info/archives/20432).

4. See David Kinnaman, *You Lost Me: Why Young Christians Are Leaving Church . . . and Rethinking Faith* (Grand Rapids: Baker, 2011), 131–48.

5. See Vincent Carroll and David Shiflett, "Christianity and Progress," Catholic Education Resource Center, www.catholiceducation.org/en/culture/history/christianity-and-progress.html.

6. Quoted in Gary DeMar, *American Christian History: The Untold Story* (Powder Springs, GA: American Vision, 1993), 102–3, italics added.

7. Particularly in Reformed traditions (see E. Digby Baltzell, *Puritan Boston and Quaker Philadelphia* [New York: Free Press, 1979], 248).

8. Dorothy L. Sayers, *Christian Letters to a Post-Christian World* (Grand Rapids: Eerdmans, 1969), 10.

9. John Wesley, "The Letters of John Wesley: To Joseph Benson, November 7, 1768," https://wesley.nnu.edu/john-wesley/the-letters-of-john-wesley/wesleys-letters-1768/#.

10. See Warren I. Susman, *Culture as History: The Transformation of American Society in the Twentieth Century* (1973; repr., New York: Pantheon, 1984). This shift is due in part to collapsing religious communities. For more, see James Davison Hunter, *The Death of Character: Moral Education in an Age Without Good or Evil* (New York: Basic Books, 2008).

11. Elisabeth Lasch-Quinn, "A Stranger's Dream: The Virtual Self and the Socialization Crisis," in *Figures in the Carpet: Finding the Human Person in the American Past*, ed. Wilfred M. McClay (Grand Rapids: Eerdmans, 2007), 236.

12. A core theme of Zephaniah's critique of prideful Assyria (see Nathan Hays, "Humility and Instruction in Zephaniah 3.1–7," *Journal for the Study of the Old Testament* 44, no. 3 [2020]: 472–89).

13. Daniel J. Estes, *Hear, My Son: Teaching and Learning in Proverbs 1–9* (Downers Grove, IL: IVP Academic, 2000), 48.

14. The double use of *didaskantes* ("to teach") for Jesus' teaching (Matthew 5:2; 7:28; 9:11, 35; 11:1) and the churches is intentional in Matthew's gospel. As the church teaches, Jesus teaches.

15. The famous, oft-contested statement by Christian philosopher Arthur F. Holmes in *All Truth Is God's Truth* (Grand Rapids: Eerdmans, 1977).

16. Augustine, *On Christian Doctrine, in Four Books*, 2.18.28, Christian Classics Ethereal Library, accessed October 2, 2024, https://ccel.org/ccel/augustine/doctrine/doctrine.xix_1.html.

17. Thomas Aquinas, *Questiones Disputatae de Veritate*, "Question 1: Truth, Article VIII." Aquinas repeatedly used this statement and gave credit for it to Ambrose, https://isidore.co/aquinas/QD deVer1.htm.

18. See Larry W. Hurtado, *Destroyer of the gods: Early Christian Distinctiveness in the Roman World* (Waco, TX: Baylor University Press, 2016).

19. Christians, Michael F. Bird and N. T. Wright contend, had "a strong book culture with an emphasis on reading sacred texts" (*The New Testament in Its World: An Introduction to the History,*

Literature, and Theology of the First Christians [Grand Rapids: Zondervan Academic, 2019], 110).

20. See Hurtado, *Destroyer of the gods*, 105–42.

21. Augustine, *The Retractations*, vol. 60 of *The Fathers of the Church*, trans. Sister Mary Inez Bogan (Washington, DC: Catholic University of America Press, 1968).

22. Ian Bradley, *The Celtic Way* (London: Darton, Longman & Todd, 1993), 70.

23. Mark Galli and Ted Olsen, eds., *131 Christians Everyone Should Know* (Nashville: Holman Reference, 2010), 322.

24. Gene Edward Veith Jr., *Loving God with All Your Mind: Thinking as a Christian in the Postmodern World* (Wheaton, IL: Crossway, 2003), 22.

25. Martin Luther, "To the Councilmen of All Cities in Germany That They Establish and Maintain Christian Schools," GodRules.net, accessed October 2, 2024, https://godrules.net /library/luther/NEW1luther_d9.htm.

26. An exhaustive look at Luther's theology and practice of education is seen in Gerald Strauss, *Luther's House of Learning: Indoctrination of the Young in the German Reformation* (Baltimore: Johns Hopkins University Press, 1978).

27. See John Calvin, "Prayer Lecture 62" on Amos, in *Commentary on Joel, Amos, Obadiah*, Christian Classics Ethereal Library, accessed October 2, 2024, www.ccel.org/ccel/c/calvin/calcom27 /cache/calcom27.pdf.

28. See Raymond A. Blacketer, "Smooth Stones, Teachable Hearts: Calvin's Allegorical Interpretation of Deuteronomy 10:1–2," *Calvin Theological Journal* 34, no. 1 (1999): 36–63.

29. See James B. Sauer, *The Teachability of the Heart: Theological Ethics in the Work of John Calvin (1509–1564)* (Ottawa, Canada: University of Ottawa Press, 1992), 133. "Teachability of the heart" was a core feature of Calvin's ethical theology.

30. On John Wesley's similar impact on "democratized learning" in Holiness traditions, see Oscar Sherwin, *John Wesley: Friend of the People* (Woodbridge, CT: Twayne, 1961), 145–46.

31. Cornelius Plantinga Jr., *Engaging God's World: A Christian Vision of Faith, Learning, and Living* (Grand Rapids: Eerdmans, 2002), x.

32. See Rodney Stark, *The Victory of Reason: How Christianity Led to Freedom, Capitalism, and Western Success* (New York: Random House, 2006), 52–53.

33. Mark A. Noll, *Jesus Christ and the Life of the Mind* (Grand Rapids: Eerdmans, 2013), xii.

34. Alister McGrath, *Mere Theology: Christian Faith and the Discipleship of the Mind* (London: SPCK, 2011), 5.

35. Donald C. Guthrie, "Faith and Teaching," in *Christian Higher Education: Faith, Teaching, and Learning in the Evangelical Tradition*, ed. David S. Dockery and Christopher W. Morgan (Wheaton, IL: Crossway, 2018), 151, italics in original.

Chapter 2: Learning from Experts

1. Compiled from Rick M. Nañez, *Full Gospel, Fractured Minds? A Call to Use God's Gift of the Intellect* (Grand Rapids: Zondervan Academic, 2005), 32; see also Gene Edward Veith Jr., *Loving God with All Your Mind: Thinking as a Christian in the Postmodern World* (Wheaton, IL: Crossway, 2003).

2. Jack Levison, *Inspired: The Holy Spirit and the Mind of Faith* (Grand Rapids: Eerdmans, 2013), 68–69.

3. The Dunning-Kruger effect is explored in chapters 1–2 of David Dunning, *Self-Insight: Roadblocks and Detours on the Path to Knowing Thyself* (New York: Psychology Press, 2005).

4. See Anders Ericsson and Robert Pool, *Peak: Secrets from the New Science of Expertise* (New York: Mariner Books, 2016). Naturally, Ericsson's work has been strongly critiqued.

5. Howard Gardner, *Creating Minds: An Anatomy of Creativity Seen Through the Lives of Freud, Einstein, Picasso, Stravinsky, Eliot, Graham, and Gandhi* (New York: Basic Books, 1993); see K. Anders Ericsson and Neil Charness, "Expert Performance: Its Structure and Acquisition," *American Psychologist* 49, no. 8 (1994): 725–47, www.chrest.info/Fribourg_Cours_Expertise/Articles -www/III%20Theories/ericsson_charness.pdf.

6. Roger Kneebone, *Expert: Understanding the Path to Mastery* (New York: Penguin, 2020), 5.

7. A paradigm suggested by Hubert Dreyfus and Stuart Dreyfus, *Mind over Machine: The Power of Human Intuition and Expertise in the Era of the Computer* (New York: Simon & Schuster, 1986).

8. Discussed throughout Michael Polanyi, *Personal Knowledge: Towards a Post-Critical Philosophy* (New York: Routledge, 2005).

9. Dallas Willard, *Knowing Christ Today: Why We Can Trust Spiritual Knowledge* (San Francisco: HarperSanFrancisco, 2009), 141.

10. Kneebone, *Expert*, 48–49. For further exploration, see Harry Collins and Robert Evans, *Rethinking Expertise* (Chicago: University of Chicago Press, 2008).

11. Tom Nichols, *The Death of Expertise: The Campaign Against Established Knowledge and Why It Matters* (Oxford: Oxford University Press, 2017).

12. As told in Parker Palmer, *The Courage to Teach: Exploring the Inner Landscape of a Teacher's Life* (San Francisco: Jossey-Bass, 1998), 59–60.

13. For an insightful, though aged, text on this theme, see Henry Zylstra, *Testament of Vision* (Grand Rapids: Eerdmans, 1958).

14. Willard, *Knowing Christ Today*, 3.

15. Mark A. Noll, *The Scandal of the Evangelical Mind* (Grand Rapids: Eerdmans, 1995).

16. Molly Worthen, *Apostles of Reason: The Crisis of Authority in American Evangelicalism* (Oxford: Oxford University Press, 2013).

17. Os Guinness, *Fit Bodies, Fat Minds: Why Evangelicals Don't Think and What to Do About It* (Grand Rapids: Baker, 1994), 8.

18. To be clear, there are many Christian luminaries in the field, including Drs. Katharine Hayhoe (Texas Tech University) and Rick Lindroth (University of Wisconsin–Madison) who furiously love Christ as environmentalists.

19. See 2 Corinthians 3:18. For a model of this kind of teachability, read Mark A. Noll, *From Every Tribe and Nation: A Historian's Discovery of the Global Christian Story* (Grand Rapids: Baker Academic, 2014).

20. Paul Tillich, *Life in the Spirit: History and the Kingdom of God*, vol. 3 of *Systematic Theology* (Chicago: University of Chicago Press, 1963), 214.

21. A. W. Tozer rightly rejected the notion that there was a "secular mind" and a "religious mind"; rather, there is only the "mind of Christ" (1 Corinthians 2:16) (*The Crucified Life: How to Live Out a Deeper Christian Experience*, ed. James L. Snyder [Minneapolis: Bethany House, 2011], 39–40).

22. See Acts 8:26–40.

23. Alister McGrath, *Mere Theology: Christian Faith and the Discipleship of the Mind* (London: SPCK, 2011), 122.

24. Willard, *Knowing Christ Today*, 7.

25. The phrase "reality is nothing but a collective hunch" is said by bag lady Lily Tomlin in Jane Wagner, *The Search for Signs of Intelligent Life in the Universe* (New York: HarperCollins, 1991); quoted in Dallas Willard's commencement speech at Azusa Pacific University in 1994 titled "Being Valiant for Truth Today."

26. Bonnie Kristian, "Can We Resurrect Expertise?," *Christianity Today*, June 21, 2022, www.christianitytoday.com/2022/06 /bonnie-kristian-resurrect-expertise-authority-trust-pride/.

27. On sin's impact on expertise, see Mark A. Noll, *Jesus Christ and the Life of the Mind* (Grand Rapids: Eerdmans, 2013), 61.

28. Aaron Jason Swoboda, *Tongues and Trees: Towards a Pentecostal Ecological Theology*, Journal of Pentecostal Theology Supplement Series 40 (Blandford Forum, UK: Deo, 2013).

29. See Clay Routledge, "Don't Believe in God? Maybe You'll Try UFOs," *New York Times*, July 21, 2017, www.nytimes.com/2017 /07/21/opinion/sunday/dont-believe-in-god-maybe-youll-try -ufos.html.

30. Gerd Theissen, *The Miracle Stories of the Early Christian Tradition*, trans. Francis McDonagh (Philadelphia: Fortress, 1983), 232.

31. See Edgar H. Schein and Peter A. Schein, *Humble Inquiry: The Gentle Art of Asking Instead of Telling* (Oakland, CA: Berrett-Koehler, 2021).

32. See George M. Marsden, "Human Depravity: A Neglected

Explanatory Category," in *Figures in the Carpet: Finding the Human Person in the American Past*, ed. Wilfred M. McClay (Grand Rapids: Eerdmans, 2003), 15–32.

33. Kristian, "Can We Resurrect Expertise?"

34. Dallas Willard, *Called to Business: God's Way of Loving People Through Business and the Professions* (Dallas Willard Ministries, 2019), 16.

Chapter 3: Learning from Strangers

1. Clark Kerr, *The Uses of the University* (Cambridge, MA: Harvard University Press, 2013), 15.

2. Found throughout Jane Jacobs, *The Death and Life of Great American Cities* (New York: Random House, 1961).

3. Erving Goffman, *Behavior in Public Places: Notes on the Social Organization of Gatherings* (New York: Free Press, 1963), 84.

4. Edward Westermarck, *The Origin and Development of the Moral Ideas*, 2nd ed. (1906; repr., London: Macmillan, 1912), 574–75.

5. Alan Gregerman, *The Necessity of Strangers: The Intriguing Truth About Insight, Innovation, and Success* (San Francisco: Jossey-Bass, 2013), 6.

6. Michael Capuzzo, *Close to Shore: The Terrifying Shark Attacks of 1916* (New York: Broadway Books, 2002).

7. Peter Singer, *The Expanding Circle: Ethics, Evolution, and Moral Progress* (1981; repr., Princeton, NJ: Princeton University Press, 2011).

8. Gregerman, *Necessity of Strangers*, 3.

9. See Apoorvaa Mandar Bichu, "What Is the Right Age for a Kid to Get a Cellphone?," Education Week, June 28, 2022, www.edweek.org/leadership/what-is-the-right-age-for-a-kid-to-get-a-cellphone/2022/06.

10. Truth-default theory is our operating assumption that people we interact with are inherently trustworthy. Malcolm Gladwell rightly points out that unearned trust of strangers can lead to abuse (see *Talking to Strangers: What We Should Know About the People We Don't Know* [New York: Little, Brown, 2019]).

11. I haven't seen Dr. Byron McCane since. But thanks for the conversation. As a result, I've changed a bunch of my lectures; see Byron R. McCane, "'Let the Dead Bury Their Own Dead'; Secondary Burial and Matt 8:21–22," *Harvard Theological Review* 83, no. 1 (January 1990): 31–43.

12. I'm grateful to have encountered this idea in Alan Jacobs, *The Pleasures of Reading in an Age of Distraction* (Oxford: Oxford University Press, 2011), 143–45.

13. "The Spirit searches all things" (1 Corinthians 2:10). In fact, Paul writes, "How unsearchable his judgments, and his paths beyond tracing out!" (Romans 11:33). We must remember that God's revelation is far different than an internet search. It is in prayer, God tells Jeremiah, that he will "tell you great and unsearchable things you do not know" (Jeremiah 33:3).

14. T. S. Eliot, *The Rock* (New York: Harcourt, Brace, 1934), 7.

15. See Gregerman, *Necessity of Strangers*, 73–75.

16. Kenneth E. Bailey, *Jesus Through Middle Eastern Eyes: Cultural Studies in the Gospels* (Downers Grove, IL: IVP Academic, 2008), 204.

17. David I. Smith, *Learning from the Stranger: Christian Faith and Cultural Diversity* (Grand Rapids: Eerdmans, 2009), 146.

18. See, for example, David Topus, *Talk to Strangers: How Everyday, Random Encounters Can Expand Your Business, Career, Income, and Life* (New York: Wiley, 2012).

19. On boundaries and loving strangers, see Miroslav Volf, "A Vision of Embrace: Theological Perspectives on Cultural Identity and Conflict," *Ecumenical Review* 48, no. 2 (April 1995): 195–205.

20. "Intellectual empathy" is borrowed from Gene C. Fant Jr., "Teaching and Learning in the Humanities," in *Christian Higher Education: Faith, Teaching, and Learning in the Evangelical Tradition*, ed. David S. Dockery and Christopher W. Morgan (Wheaton, IL: Crossway, 2018), 205–24. "Intellectual hospitality" is a phrase of Diana Pavlac Glyer, "Intellectual Hospitality," Azusa Pacific University, July 21, 2015, www.apu.edu/articles/intellectual-hospitality/.

21. Gabriel García Márquez, "The Handsomest Drowned Man in the World," in *Leaf Storm and Other Stories* (New York: Harper & Row, 1972).

22. Better known as "inattentional blindness." For more, see Christopher Chabris and Daniel Simons, *The Invisible Gorilla: And Other Ways Our Intuitions Deceive Us* (New York: Crown, 2010), 1–42.

23. See Saul McLeod, "Fundamental Attribution Error in Psychology," Simply Psychology, updated June 15, 2023, www.simplypsychology.org/fundamental-attribution.html.

24. Gladwell, *Talking to Strangers*, 50.

25. Umberto Eco, *Serendipities: Language and Lunacy* (New York: Columbia University Press, 1999), 54.

26. See the story of the angels who visit Abraham and Sarah in Genesis 18.

27. Richard Beck, *Stranger God: Meeting Jesus in Disguise* (Minneapolis: Fortress, 2017), 27.

28. Kathleen Norris, *Dakota: A Spiritual Geography* (1993; repr., New York: Mariner, 2001), 191. A nod to Eugene Peterson, who introduced me to this little book in *Tell It Slant: A Conversation on the Language of Jesus in His Stories and Prayers* (Grand Rapids: Eerdmans, 2012).

29. See Jeremiah Unterman, *Justice for All: How the Jewish Bible Revolutionized Ethics* (Lincoln: University of Nebraska Press, 2017).

30. "Quartet of the vulnerable" is used throughout Nicholas Wolterstorff, *Justice: Rights and Wrongs* (Princeton, NJ: Princeton University Press, 2008).

31. Notably, the Old Testament quotes the Book of Jashar as a text of wisdom (Joshua 10:12–13; 2 Samuel 1:18). Similarly, the book of Jude quotes the noncanonical text of Enoch (Jude 14–15).

32. Bill Donahue, *The Irresistible Community: An Invitation to Life Together* (Grand Rapids: Baker, 2015), 29.

33. David I. Smith and Barbara Carvill, *The Gift of the Stranger:*

Faith, Hospitality, and Foreign Language Learning (Grand Rapids: Eerdmans, 2000), 91–92.

34. Richard Sennett, *The Fall of Public Man* (1974; repr., New York: Norton, 1991), 39.

35. Sennett's thought is surveyed in Justin McGuirk, "Can Cities Make Us Better Citizens?," *The New Yorker*, April 26, 2018, www.newyorker.com/books/page-turner/can-cities-make-us -better-citizens.

36. Joe Keohane, *The Power of Strangers: The Benefits of Connecting in a Suspicious World* (New York: Random House, 2021), xiii.

37. Bailey, *Jesus Through Middle Eastern Eyes*, 201–2.

38. Thomas W. Ogletree, *Hospitality to the Stranger: Dimensions of Moral Understanding* (Louisville, KY: Westminster John Knox, 2003), 2–3.

39. John Calvin, *Institutes of the Christian Religion*, vol. 1, ed. John T. McNeill (Philadelphia: Westminster, 1960), 43–44 (1.3.1).

Chapter 4: Learning from the Dead

1. See Ernest Becker, *The Denial of Death* (New York: Free Press, 1973).

2. See Lewis Mumford, *The Culture of Cities* (Westport, CT: Greenwood, 1981).

3. Charles J. Reid Jr., "The Disposal of the Dead: And What It Tells Us About American Society and Law," in *Figures in the Carpet: Finding the Person in the American Past*, ed. Wilfred M. McClay (Grand Rapids: Eerdmans, 2007), 443.

4. Lore Ferguson Wilbert, *The Understory: An Invitation to Rootedness and Resilience from the Forest Floor* (Grand Rapids: Brazos, 2024), 90.

5. See McClay, *Figures in the Carpet*, 430.

6. See McClay, *Figures in the Carpet*, 430.

7. Anecdotally told by Fr. Ronald Rolheiser, "How to Truly Love Yourself," The Church in the 21st Century Center, Boston College, March 27, 2017, YouTube video, 57:59, www.youtube .com/watch?v=9fdl3VEOxng.

8. Dallas Willard, "Nietzsche Versus Jesus Christ," in *A Place for Truth: Leading Thinkers Explore Life's Hardest Questions*, ed. Dallas Willard (Downers Grove, IL: InterVarsity, 2010), 159.

9. Bradley P. Holt, *Thirsty for God: A Brief History of Christian Spirituality* (Minneapolis: Fortress, 2017), 18.

10. C. S. Lewis, *Surprised by Joy: The Shape of My Early Life* (New York: Harcourt, Brace, 1955), 201.

11. Forcefully argued throughout Eric Voegelin, *Order and History: Israel and Revelation*, vol. 1 (Baton Rouge: Louisiana State University Press, 1956).

12. Francis Schaeffer, *The Complete Works of Francis Schaeffer*, vol. 1 (Wheaton, IL: Crossway, 1994), 147.

13. Robert N. Bellah et al., *Habits of the Heart: Individualism and Commitment in American Life* (Berkeley: University of California Press, 1985), 153.

14. A resounding theme throughout Ellen T. Charry, *By the Renewing of Your Minds: The Pastoral Function of Christian Doctrine* (New York: Oxford University Press, 1999).

15. Mark Schwehn, *Exiles from Eden: Religion and the Academic Vocation in America* (New York: Oxford University Press, 1993), 48, italics in original.

16. See Charles Taylor, *Hegel* (New York: Cambridge University Press, 1975), 6.

17. Augusto Del Noce, *The Crisis of Modernity*, trans. Carlos Lancellotti (London: McGill-Queen's University Press, 2014), 127.

18. For a poignant exploration of celebrity Christianity, see Katelyn Beaty, *Celebrities for Jesus: How Personas, Platforms, and Profits Are Hurting the Church* (Grand Rapids: Brazos, 2022).

19. Joshua D. Chatraw and Jack Carson, *Surprised by Doubt: How Disillusionment Can Invite Us into a Deeper Faith* (Grand Rapids: Brazos, 2023), 11.

20. C. S. Lewis, introduction to Athanasius, *On the Incarnation*, (1944; repr., Crestwood, NY: St. Vladimir's Seminary Press, 1993), 4.

21. Lewis, introduction, 4.

22. See Jason Hood, *Imitating God in Christ: Recapturing a Biblical Pattern* (Downers Grove, IL: IVP Academic, 2013).

23. See Thomas à Kempis, *The Imitation of Christ* (Mineola, NY: Dover, 2003).

24. See "Post-Mortems vs Retrospectives: What's the Difference?," Parabol, accessed October 26, 2024, www.parabol.co/blog /retrospectives-vs-post-mortems/.

25. Paul R. House, *Old Testament Theology* (Downers Grove, IL: IVP Academic, 1998), 266.

26. A paraphrase of Matthew 16:18.

27. Stanley Fish, *Is There a Text in This Class? The Authority of Interpretive Communities* (Cambridge, MA: Harvard University Press, 1982).

28. Stanley Hauerwas, *Unleashing the Scripture: Freeing the Bible from Captivity to America* (Nashville: Abingdon, 1993), 15.

29. Rodney Clapp, *A Peculiar People: The Church as Culture in a Post-Christian Society* (Downers Grove, IL: InterVarsity, 1996), 130.

30. See, for example, Exodus 13:9, 14, 16; 16:6; 18:1.

31. Charry, *Renewing of Your Minds*, viii.

32. Jaroslav Pelikan, *The Vindication of Tradition* (New Haven, CT: Yale University Press, 1984), 65.

33. John L. Thompson, *Reading the Bible with the Dead: What You Can Learn from the History of Exegesis That You Can't Learn from Exegesis Alone* (Grand Rapids: Eerdmans, 2007), 6.

34. G. K. Chesterton, *Orthodoxy* (1908; repr., Mineola, NY: Dover, 2020), 40.

35. Alister McGrath points out that both Cyril of Jerusalem (313–386) and Vladimir Lossky (1903–1958) described catholicity as a kind of collaboration (*Mere Theology: Christian Faith and the Discipleship of the Mind* [London: SPCK, 2011], 7).

36. W. H. Auden, *The Complete Works of W. H. Auden: Prose, Volume V: 1963–1968*, ed. Edward Mendelson (Princeton, NJ: Princeton University Press, 2015), 477.

Chapter 5: Learning from Children

1. And this is, in fact, the name of a weekly devotional I write called "The Low-Level Theologian," which can be found at https://ajswoboda.substack.com/.

2. Second Peter 3:15–16 evidences Peter's willingness to endorse and enfranchise the writings and thinking of the newer Christian Paul.

3. Scot McKnight and Laura Barringer, *A Church Called Tov: Forming a Goodness Culture That Resists Abuses of Power and Promotes Healing* (Carol Stream, IL: Tyndale Elevate, 2020), 135.

4. I'm grateful for a providential conversation I had with my friend Dr. Richard Beck, who nudged me toward this insight in psychological history. Despite it, I admit my continued contempt for much of Freud's thought.

5. See Jerome W. Berryman, *Children and the Theologians: Clearing the Way for Grace* (New York: Morehouse, 2009), 54–59.

6. This section's materials on Einstein are drawn from Walter Isaacson, *Einstein: His Life and Universe* (New York: Simon & Schuster, 2008), 347, 439–40.

7. On the absence of children in theology, see Donald Ratcliff, "Children's Spirituality: Past and Future," *Journal of Spiritual Formation and Soul Care* 3, no. 1 (May 2010): 6–20.

8. See O. M. Bakke, *When Children Became People: The Birth of Childhood in Early Christianity* (Minneapolis: Fortress, 2005), 260–79.

9. Research even suggests that children commonly have "numinous experiences" with God but often don't report them. See Donald Ratcliff, ed., *Children's Spirituality: Christian Perspectives, Research, and Applications* (Eugene, OR: Cascade Books, 2004).

10. Earl Barnes, "Theological Life of a California Child," *The Pedagogical Seminary* 2, no. 3 (1892): 442–48, www.tandfonline.com/doi/abs/10.1080/08919402.1982.10532892.

11. Berryman, *Children and the Theologians*, 2–3.

12. See Marcia J. Bunge, Terence E. Fretheim, and Beverly Roberts Gaventa, *The Child in the Bible* (Grand Rapids: Eerdmans,

2008). Another great example is David M. Csinos, *Little Theologians: Children, Culture, and the Making of Theological Meaning* (Montreal: McGill-Queen's University Press, 2020).

13. See Haddon Willmer, "What Is 'Child Theology'?," in *Toddling to the Kingdom: Child Theology at Work in the Church*, ed. John Collier (London: Child Theology Movement, 2009), 23–27.

14. See Faith Karimi, "The First Social Media Babies Are Adults Now. Some Are Pushing for Laws to Protect Kids from Their Parents' Oversharing," CNN, May 29, 2024, www.cnn.com/20 24/05/29/us/social-media-children-influencers-cec/index.html.

15. Carl G. Jung, "The Significance of the Father in the Destiny of the Individual," in *Freud and Psychoanalysis*, vol. 4 (New York: Routledge, 2015), 301–23.

16. Andy Crouch, "Promises, Promises," *Christianity Today* 45, no. 3 (February 19, 2001), https://andy-crouch.com/articles/promises _promises.

17. Tom Wright, "Letters to the Editor: Gender-Fluid World," *The Times*, August 3, 2017, www.thetimes.com/article/energy -tariffs-and-the-wisdom-of-a-price-cap-6nnszcfds.

18. Mary Stewart Van Leeuwen, *Gender and Grace: Love, Work, and Parenting in a Changing World* (Downers Grove, IL: InterVarsity, 1990), 49.

19. Berryman, *Children and the Theologians*, 17, italics mine.

20. As Grant Macaskill points out, *humility* and *poor* or *poverty* are lexically connected in the Bible ("Christian Scriptures and the Formation of Intellectual Humility," *Journal of Psychology and Theology* 46, no. 4 [November 2018]: 243–52).

21. On this discipline of learning humility, see Richard J. Foster, *Learning Humility: A Year of Searching for a Vanishing Virtue* (Downers Grove, IL: InterVarsity, 2022).

22. On the science of reading to children, see Dee Reid and Diana Bentley, *Help Your Child to Read: A Teach Yourself Guide* (Chicago: McGraw Hill, 2010).

23. See Brandon T. McDaniel and Sarah M. Coyne, "'Technoference': The Interference of Technology in Couple Relationships and

Implications for Women's Personal and Relational Well-Being," *Psychology of Popular Media Culture* 5, no. 1 (2016): 85–98, https://scholarsarchive.byu.edu/cgi/viewcontent.cgi?article=5003 &context=facpub.

24. See Pamela Gerloff, "You're Not Laughing Enough, and That's No Joke," *Psychology Today*, June 21, 2011, www.psychology today.com/us/blog/the-possibility-paradigm/201106/youre-not -laughing-enough-and-thats-no-joke.

25. Ronald Rolheiser, *Against an Infinite Horizon: The Finger of God in Our Everyday Lives* (New York: Crossroad, 2001), 31.

26. See Marjorie Taylor, *Imaginary Companions and the Children Who Create Them* (New York: Oxford University Press, 1999), 37, 65.

27. John Webster, "On the Theology of the Intellectual Life," in *Christ Across the Disciplines: Past, Present, Future*, ed. Roger Lundin (Grand Rapids: Eerdmans, 2013), 111, italics in original.

28. Cited in Casey Tygrett, *Becoming Curious: A Spiritual Practice of Asking Questions* (Downers Grove, IL: InterVarsity, 2017), 29.

29. Lyle W. Dorsett and Marjorie Lamp Mead, eds., *C. S. Lewis' Letters to Children* (New York: Touchstone, 1995). For an overview of Lewis's writings to children, see S. D. Smith, "C. S. Lewis's Wonderful Letters to Children," Story Warren, May 30, 2018, https://storywarren.com/c-s-lewiss-wonderful -letters-to-children/.

30. C. S. Lewis, *Mere Christianity* (1943; repr., New York: Macmillan, 1960), 75.

Chapter 6: Learning from Parents

1. William Breault, "'I Am Not Worthy to Have You Come Under My Roof' (Matthew 8:8)," in *Hearts on Fire: Praying with Jesuits*, ed. Michael Harter (Chicago: Loyola, 2005), 45.

2. See Carl Rogers, *Freedom to Learn: A View of What Education Might Become* (Columbus, OH: Merrill, 1969).

3. This topic is explored at length in D. W. Winnicott, *Family and Individual Development* (New York: Routledge, 2021).

4. John Calvin, *Institutes of the Christian Religion*, vol. 1, ed. John T. McNeill (Philadelphia: Westminster, 1960), 121 (1.13.1).

5. Elisabeth Lasch-Quinn, "A Stranger's Dream: The Virtual Self and the Socialization Crisis," in *Figures in the Carpet: Finding the Human Person in the American Past*, ed. Wilfred M. McClay (Grand Rapids: Eerdmans, 2007), 252.

6. Philip Rieff, *The Triumph of the Therapeutic: Uses of Faith After Freud* (Chicago: University of Chicago Press, 1987), 243.

7. Richard J. Herrnstein and Charles Murray, *The Bell Curve: Intelligence and Class Structure in American Life* (1994; repr., New York: Free Press, 2010), 91.

8. See Eleanor A. Maguire et al., "Navigation-Related Structural Change in the Hippocampi of Taxi Drivers," *Proceedings of the National Academy of Sciences* 97, no. 8 (April 2000): 4398–4403, www.pnas.org/doi/10.1073/pnas.070039597.

9. David Shenk, *The Genius in All of Us: Why Everything You've Been Told About Genetics, Talent and IQ Is Wrong* (New York: Doubleday, 2010), 8, italics in original.

10. See Ewen Callaway, "Fearful Memories Haunt Mouse Descendants," *Nature*, December 1, 2013, 1–6, www.nature.com /articles/nature.2013.14272.

11. See Christopher Milne, *The Path Through the Trees* (Bristol, UK: Policy Press, 2014).

12. National Scientific Council on the Developing Child, *Children's Emotional Development Is Built into the Architecture of Their Brains: Working Paper 2*, Center on the Developing Child, Harvard University (2004), https://developingchild.harvard.edu/wp -content/uploads/2024/10/Childrens-Emotional-Development-Is -Built-into-the-Architecture-of-Their-Brains.pdf.

13. See, e.g., 2 Kings 21:20; 23:37; 24:9 (among others).

14. E. D. Hirsch Jr,, *Cultural Literacy: What Every American Needs to Know* (New York: Vintage, 1987), xvi.

15. Barry Sanders, *A Is for Ox: The Collapse of Literacy and the Rise of Violence in an Electronic Age* (New York: Vintage, 1995), 44.

16. See the story of Lewis and Janie Moore, his "adopted mother," throughout A. N. Wilson, *C. S. Lewis: A Biography* (1990; repr., New York: Norton, 2002), esp. 92–95.

17. A resounding theme throughout Ellen T. Charry, *By the Renewing of Your Minds: The Pastoral Function of Christian Doctrine* (New York: Oxford University Press, 1999).

18. Karl Barth, *The Word of God and the Word of Man* (New York: Harper & Row, 1957), 196.

19. For me, the best theological account for this component of Christ's humanity is found in chapter 2 of R. Michael Allen, *The Christ's Faith: A Dogmatic Account* (London: Bloomsbury, 2011), 36–68.

20. From a helpful lecture, "The Book of Hebrews with Dr. George Guthrie: Theology, Ethics, Background, and Structure," THE CHARGE with Dennis Metzler, June 26, 2022, YouTube video, 1:06:47, www.youtube.com/watch?v=teqNX9kCaeA.

Chapter 7: Learning from Secular Culture

1. Kelvin Crow and Mark Galli, "Wordly Monk," *Christian History* 64 (1999), https://christianhistoryinstitute.org/magazine/article/wordly-monk#.

2. Michael J. Gorman, *Reading Revelation Responsibly: Uncivil Worship and Witness: Following the Lamb into the New Creation* (Eugene, OR: Cascade Books, 2011), 31–32.

3. Tertullian, *The Prescription Against Heretics*, Christian Classics Ethereal Library, accessed October 29, 2024, https://ccel.org/ccel/tertullian/heretics/anf03.v.iii.vii.html.

4. Flannery O'Connor, *The Habit of Being: Letters of Flannery O'Connor*, ed. Sally Fitzgerald (New York: Farrar, Straus and Giroux, 1979), 477.

5. Clark H. Pinnock, *Flame of Love: A Theology of the Holy Spirit* (Downers Grove, IL: InterVarsity, 1996), 203.

6. Richard J. Mouw, *Consulting the Faithful: What Christian Intellectuals Can Learn from Popular Religion* (Grand Rapids: Eerdmans, 1994), 10–11.

7. Mouw, *Consulting the Faithful*, 11.

8. A helpful resource on this distinction is Robert Johnston, *God's Wider Presence: Reconsidering General Revelation* (Grand Rapids: Baker Academic, 2014).

9. On Calvin's view of revelation through culture, see Cornelius Plantinga Jr., *Engaging God's World: A Christian Vision of Faith, Learning, and Living* (Grand Rapids: Eerdmans, 2002).

10. See Paul Louis Metzger, *The Word of Christ and the World of Culture: Sacred and Secular Through the Theology of Karl Barth* (Eugene, OR: Wipf & Stock, 2005), 3–36.

11. The two phrases are tied to the final discourse in John, where Jesus sends the disciples "into the world" (17:18) but tells them to "not belong to the world" (15:19).

12. Jürgen Moltmann, *The Crucified God* (London: SCM Press, 1974), 29.

13. See Rodney Stark, *One True God: Historical Consequences of Monotheism* (Princeton, NJ: Princeton University Press, 2001), 67–69.

14. See Harold A. Netland and Keith E. Johnson, "Why Is Religious Pluralism Fun—and Dangerous?," in *Telling the Truth: Evangelizing Postmoderns*, ed. D. A. Carson (Grand Rapids: Zondervan, 2000), 47.

15. For more, see the masterful Robert J. Banks, *Paul's Idea of Community: Spirit and Culture in Early House Churches* (Grand Rapids: Baker Academic, 2020).

16. Nijay K. Gupta, *Tell Her Story: How Women Led, Taught, and Ministered in the Early Church* (Downers Grove, IL: IVP Academic, 2023), 75–81.

17. As does Michael Frost, who envisions learning as a key attribute of a church on mission. See chapter 6 of Michael Frost, *Surprise the World: The Five Habits of Highly Missional People* (Colorado Springs: NavPress, 2016), 71–84.

18. See James C. Scott, *Domination and the Arts of Resistance: Hidden Transcripts* (New Haven, CT: Yale University Press, 2008).

19. See Richard J. Mouw, *Called to Holy Worldliness* (Philadelphia: Fortress, 1980), 46–47.

20. I was introduced to this idea in Sandra McCracken, "Our Two Spiritual Time Zones," *Christianity Today*, August 18, 2017, www.sandramccracken.com/christianity-today-writings/2020/9 /12/our-two-spiritual-time-zones.

21. Gerald G. May, *The Awakened Heart: Opening Yourself to the Love You Need* (San Francisco: HarperSanFrancisco, 1991), 154.

22. Nicholas Wolterstorff, *Reason Within the Bounds of Religion* (Grand Rapids: Eerdmans, 1976), 66.

23. John D. Woodbridge, "The Authority of Holy Scripture," in *Christian Higher Education: Faith, Teaching, and Learning in the Evangelical Tradition*, ed. David S. Dockery and Christopher W. Morgan (Wheaton, IL: Crossway, 2018), 61.

24. John Wesley, *The Works of the Rev. John Wesley, A.M.*, vol. 6 (New York: Emory & Waugh, 1831), 750.

25. Ignatius, "Letter to the Trallians," in *Early Christian Fathers*, ed. Cyril C. Richardson (Philadelphia: Westminster, 1953), 100, www.ccel.org/ccel/richardson/fathers.vi.ii.iii.iii.html.

26. Famously articulated by Frank Gaebelein, who said that academics often feel a pressure to bend to the ideological demands and expectations of the academy (*The Pattern of God's Truth: The Integration of Faith and Learning* [Chicago: Moody, 1973], 39).

27. Kurt Aland, *A History of Christianity: From the Beginnings to the Threshold of the Reformation*, vol. 1, trans. James L. Schaaf, (Minneapolis: Fortress, 1985), 53.

28. Rodney Stark, *The Rise of Christianity: How the Obscure, Marginal Jesus Movement Became the Dominant Religious Force in the Western World in a Few Centuries* (San Francisco: HarperSanFrancisco, 1996), 161–62, italics in original.

29. This list is informed and structured by J. P. Moreland, *Love Your God with All Your Mind: The Role of Reason in the Life of the Soul* (Colorado Springs: NavPress, 2012), 54–55.

30. See Dean Pinter, *Acts*, The Story of God Bible Commentary Series, ed. Tremper Longman III and Scot McKnight (Grand Rapids: Zondervan Academic, 2019), 564.

31. See Frank C. Senn, *Christian Worship and Its Cultural Setting*

(Eugene, OR: Wipf & Stock, 2004), 39–40. This is why
Andrew Walls famously argues that the center of Christianity
keeps changing—for good reason. It's a movement that can
find its center anywhere (*The Missionary Movement in Christian
History: Studies in the Transmission of Faith* [Maryknoll, NY:
Orbis Books, 1996], 16–25).

32. For Augustine's discussion, see *Teaching Christianity (De
Doctrina Christiana)*, in *The Works of Saint Augustine*, 1/11,
ed. John E. Rotelle (Hyde Park, NY: New City, 2007), 170.
I'm grateful for the reference in Joshua D. Chatraw and Jack
Carson, *Surprised by Doubt: How Disillusionment Can Invite
Us into a Deeper Faith* (Grand Rapids: Brazos, 2023), for
their reference to both Andrew Walls's book and Augustine's
Teaching Christianity.

33. Expressed in the most beautiful way possible in Mark
J. Cartledge, "Spirit-Empowered 'Walking Alongside': Towards
a Renewal Theology of Public Life," *Journal of Pentecostal
Theology* 27, no. 1 (March 2018): 14–36.

Chapter 8: Learning from Enemies

1. Lesslie Newbigin, *The Good Shepherd: Meditations on Christian
Ministry in Today's World* (Grand Rapids: Eerdmans, 1977), 114.

2. C. S. Lewis, *An Experiment in Criticism* (Cambridge: Cambridge
University Press, 1992), 85.

3. Quoted in Jon M. Sweeney, *My Life in Seventeen Books:
A Literary Memoir* (Rhinebeck, NY: Monkfish, 2024).

4. Antonin Scalia, *Scalia Speaks: Reflections on Law, Faith, and Life
Well Lived* (New York: Crown Forum, 2017).

5. Eugene H. Peterson, *The Wisdom of Each Other: A Conversation
Between Spiritual Friends* (Grand Rapids: Zondervan, 1998), 26.

6. *More Perfect Illustrations for Every Topic and Occasion* (Carol
Stream, IL: Tyndale, 2003), 121.

7. Emmanuel Levinas, *Difficult Freedom: Essays on Judaism*
(Baltimore: Johns Hopkins University Press, 1990), 10.

8. Jonathan Rauch, *The Constitution of Knowledge: A Defense of*

Truth (Washington, DC: Brookings Institution Press, 2021), 27, 31–34.

9. Rauch, *Constitution of Knowledge*, 166. Another great read is David E. Fitch, *The Church of Us vs. Them: Freedom from a Faith That Feeds on Making Enemies* (Grand Rapids: Brazos, 2019).

10. Quoted in Ed Kilgore, "Donald Trump Jr. Rejects Christianity's 'Turn the Other Cheek' Teaching," Intelligencer, December 27, 2021, https://nymag.com/intelligencer/2021/12/donald-trump -jr-rejects-jesuss-turn-the-other-cheek.html, italics in original.

11. Doris Kearns Goodwin, *Team of Rivals: The Political Genius of Abraham Lincoln* (New York: Simon & Schuster, 2006), 280.

12. Robert W. Funk, *Honest to God: Jesus for a New Millennium* (San Francisco: HarperSanFrancisco, 1996), 203.

13. For more on this idea, see Craig L. Blomberg, *Contagious Holiness: Jesus' Meals with Sinners* (Downers Grove, IL: InterVarsity, 2005), esp. 97–129.

14. Denis Minns and Paul Parvis, eds., *Justin, Philosopher and Martyr: Apologies* (New York: Oxford University Press, 2009), 113.

15. See Preston Sprinkle, *Nonviolence: The Revolutionary Way of Jesus* (Colorado Springs: Cook, 2021), 202.

16. See Dietrich Bonhoeffer, *Ethics* (1955; repr., New York: Touchstone, 1995), 33.

17. See Martin Luther King Jr., *Strength to Love* (Boston: Beacon, 1963).

18. See Miroslav Volf, *Exclusion and Embrace: A Theological Exploration of Identity, Otherness, and Reconciliation* (Nashville: Abingdon, 1996).

19. James K. A. Smith, "In Praise of Boredom," *Image*, no. 99, accessed October 29, 2024, https://imagejournal.org/article/in -praise-of-boredom/, italics in original.

20. Martin Luther King Jr., *A Time to Break Silence: The Essential Works of Martin Luther King, Jr., for Students* (Boston: Beacon, 2013), 19–20.

21. Here I borrow from Richard J. Mouw, *Called to Holy Worldliness* (Philadelphia: Fortress, 1980), 63–64.

22. Alan Jacobs, *How to Think: A Survival Guide for a World at Odds* (New York: Currency, 2017), 75.

23. Quoted in Jim Wilder, *Renovated: God, Dallas Willard, and the Church That Transforms* (Colorado Springs: NavPress, 2020), 3.

24. Dallas Willard, *The Divine Conspiracy: Rediscovering Our Hidden Life in God* (San Francisco: HarperSanFrancisco, 1998), 151.

25. See Nicholas Kristof, "How Can You Hate Me When You Don't Even Know Me?," *New York Times*, June 26, 2021, www.nytimes.com/2021/06/26/opinion/racism-politics-daryl-davis.html; Dwane Brown, "How One Man Convinced 200 Ku Klux Klan Members to Give Up Their Robes," NPR, August 20, 2017, www.npr.org/2017/08/20/544861933/how-one-man-convinced-200-ku-klux-klan-members-to-give-up-their-robes.

26. Gastón Espinosa, *William J. Seymour and the Origins of Global Pentecostalism: A Biography and Documentary History* (Durham, NC: Duke University Press, 2014); see also Zach Bardon, "William Seymour and the Original Pentecostal Movement," www.zachbardon.com/compendium/out.php?t=academic/Seymour.

Conclusion

1. C. S. Lewis, "Learning in War-Time: A Sermon Preached in the Church of St. Mary the Virgin, Oxford, Autumn, 1939," www.christendom.edu/wp-content/uploads/2021/02/Learning-In-Wartime-C.S.-Lewis-1939.pdf.

2. Quoted in Paul Spears, "Repairing the Ruins," The Scriptorium Daily, March 1, 2007, https://scriptoriumdaily.com/repairing-the-ruins/.

3. Noah benShea, *Jacob the Baker: Gentle Wisdom for a Complicated World* (New York: Ballantine, 1989). I'm grateful to have discovered this story in Norris Friesen and Wendy Soderquist Togami, "Collaboration: To Labor Together," in *The Soul of a Christian University: A Field Guide for Educators*, ed. Stephen T. Beers (Abilene, TX: Abilene Christian University Press, 2008), 117–28.